UNCONDITIONING
and
EDUCATION

Volume

(2)

The Need for a
Radical Approach

J. Krishnamurti

Unconditioning and Education Volume 2

Printed in the United States of America.

Published by Krishnamurti Foundation of America
PO Box 1560
Ojai, California 93024
United States of America

ISBN No. 978-0-692-96617-4

Edited by Ray McCoy and Duncan Toms

For further information about J. Krishnamurti please visit:
www.jkrishnamurti.org

CONTENTS

FOREWORD

THE EDITORS

In the lifetime of J. Krishnamurti, the last school that began with his help was in the town of Ojai in California. He had first spent time there in 1922 and, after 1933, stayed the longest continuous periods of his life in the valley. Since the early 1930s, large numbers of people attended his public talks in the town; families moved there because of their interest in what he said. It was in Ojai that he wrote his first major book, Education and the Significance of Life, published in 1953. The possibility of starting a school in his name had been mentioned from time to time after 1953, but there was no concerted movement for it until friends who had formed the Krishnamurti Foundation of America began serious discussions with him about his views on right education.

In 1970, in one of his recorded conversations with himself, Krishnamurti asked:

Could not the intelligent minority of parents get together

and start a school in which the whole of man is considered and cared for, in which the educator is not merely the informant, a machine which imparts knowledge, but is concerned with the well-being of the whole human being? ... It means creating a place where the educator is being educated, and the help of a few parents who are deeply interested. (From Beginnings of Learning, first published by Victor Gollancz Ltd in 1975.)

It may have been with this in mind that Krishnamurti agreed to meet with some trustees of KFA and other friends, first in Malibu in 1974, and continuing with parents, trustees and prospective teachers in Ojai in 1975, to discuss starting a school. The two volumes of Unconditioning and Education present these remarkable dialogues, which led to the opening of Oak Grove School in 1976.

Krishnamurti begins the discussions by explaining that traditional education prepares children to conform to society, to memorize facts in order to acquire knowledge. He says that this limits the mind by narrowing its function and limiting its creativity. The educators and the children are conditioned to traditional patterns of inquiry, neglecting exploration of broader development as whole human beings psychologically, spiritually, intellectually and morally. He would have the educators explore the possibility of bringing about a different kind of mind.

Krishnamurti asks the bold question: 'Is there a method to uncondition the human mind?' He suggests that the conditioning of tradition and society can be 'uncovered and dissolved'. He wants the parents to be involved in obedience, acceptance: you are my authority and I follow you because I am frightened. Discipline means to learn, not to revolt, not to react to what you already have been conditioned to.

In Latin, the root meaning of the word school is leisure. Leisure is necessary to learn, otherwise you cannot learn. Freedom implies responsibility; you cannot be free if you are irresponsible. You are responsible for learning, for understanding what it means to learn.

We have started a school on a very small scale with that intention. Not intention, that is what we are going to do. And to do that properly, wisely and sanely, parents must cooperate. If they come to the school, the staff will discuss with them if they want. We will discuss what it means to teach, what the teacher's function is; and whether they talk and teach from an authority, from a pedestal, or teach in relationship with the student so that, in any subject the teacher not only discusses the subject but also, in the very discussion, unconditions himself as well as the student. It is a mutual process. It is not that the teacher must first be unconditioned and then teaches. They do it together.

We want to bring about a totally different kind of mind, a mind that is intelligent, that can meet every challenge, not just isolated ones. To do that, you must understand what it means to be religious. Religion now has become organized propaganda of belief, and therefore is not religion at all. The root meaning of religion is to gather all your energy to discover what truth is, to understand what truth is, to see what truth is—which has nothing whatsoever to do with rituals, dogma, beliefs, and hierarchical priesthoods and so on. And you must understand what it means not to be afraid; what it means to understand the whole social structure, which is based on pleasure. In the pursuit of pleasure you will invariably cultivate fear. And we will go into the question of what love is.

So it is not only the academic side, but the cultivation, the understanding of the whole human mind—the student as well as the educator—so that when the child goes out from the school he has a mind that is a really good mind, a good heart—if I can use that word without becoming sentimental and romantic—and be a really religious human being. This is what we want to do.

Questioner (Q): Could you go into the idea of fear, of raising these children without the conditioning of fear? If they're going home every day to their parents...

K: That is just it. They come for eight hours to the school where there is no fear: no scolding, no giving marks, no competition, where each is as good as the others in the sense of no comparison. In the schools in India and at Brockwood, we have tried to make the student understand that learning is important, not how much he or she learns through competition, but that learning is a sacred thing. Among the Greeks as well as the Hindus there was the idea that learning is the highest quality; not just learning from books, but learning about yourself, learning how to live properly, learning what relationship is, learning about what love is, what death is. All that. So, when the students come for eight hours to the school and go back to the parents, the parents are going to have a very difficult time. That is why it is very important that we all meet together and understand what we are

Let's discuss the place of knowledge in society. What place has knowledge in society? It has helped man to function technologically, to earn a livelihood, to kill, to destroy species of animals. And that very knowledge has helped him to conform to a pattern. It is not that he must be against pattern, but understand what the pattern is and the need to change the pattern. Now, what is knowledge? What is it to know? What does it mean when I say, 'I know you'?

I know you because I met you last year or the year before. The memory of it, the picture, the face, the form is imprinted on the brain. And that is the past. So all knowledge—divine knowledge or scientific knowledge or book knowledge—is the past. There is no knowledge of tomorrow; "knowledge" of tomorrow is a projection from the known of yesterday. So, has knowledge a place in the transformation of man?

Knowledge has a place in the technological world: how to drive a car, how to speak a language, work in a factory, be a professor. Knowledge is necessary—but has knowledge changed, transformed man? Apparently it has not. This is a subject which we discussed with prominent scientists at Brockwood. The question was put to them whether knowledge has any significance in relation to the transformation of man. Apparently, knowledge has not transformed man psychologically, inwardly.

So one must go into the question: is learning merely the acquisition of knowledge? Or has learning a different meaning? If I accumulate knowledge in order to live skilfully, effectively, in a society which is corrupt, knowledge is useful there, but will that knowledge change my relationship to my wife, to my neighbour, to the world? Apparently it has not done so. So what place has knowledge? We have to go into what learning implies. As it is now understood, it is gathering information, accumulating knowledge and acting on that. That has not transformed man. It may have modified man, but it has not radically transformed him. So, knowledge has its place, but knowledge cannot transform man. Therefore some other energy is needed to transform man.

Q: So knowledge and conditioning would be almost the same.

K: Yes sir.

Q: If the educators bring this inner thing up with the students, who educates the parents?

K: We are doing it now.

Q: I can foresee a parent being totally ostracized.

K: No sir. That is what is happening in the world. But here we are asking the parents to come in. We say, 'Look, this is what we are doing, please share with us'.

Q: You are trying to create an environment in the school and at home.

K: That is right. Otherwise you destroy the child.

Q: You talked about knowledge and how that does not do what it should for man. So it is an inner thing that we need. It is understanding.

K: It requires a lot of going into. One has to go into

Q: So it is sensation plus conditioning, then.

K: No, no. Thought is the factor of conditioning, not sensation.

Q: That is what I am saying. It is sensation plus conditioning. But what sensation do we get from seeing the piano if it is not modified by the thought of what the piano is and knowing the piano?

K: No sir. I see a beautiful car: perception, sensation.

Q: That is sensation.

K: Quite right, that is sensation.

Q: As soon as I know it, that is thought.

K: That is what happens. You are perfectly right. There is sensation; then thought comes and all the trouble begins.

We are examining what desire is. We said desire is sensation plus thought. So what is thought? What is thinking? Not thinking about something, what is thinking? Isn't it memory? What is memory? Accumulated experience, stored up in the brain. I am not a brain specialist; I observe. So thought is the response of memory, which is experience, accumulated, stored up in the brain. So thought is a material process. Thought, whatever it has created, is a material process. Thought itself is material.

Q: Thought is matter.

K: No, please, we have to go slowly. Look, I met you yesterday, last week. It is stored up in the brain as memory; it is there, inside the head, in the brain. The brain is composed of many cells, matter, material processes. So the brain contains the whole structure of memory. It records and holds it. That is a fact. All these are facts, sir. So what thought has created—all the churches, all the temples, all the mosques—are material processes. There is nothing holy about them. This is very important. Thought plus sensation is desire. Desire has created all this. Wait, wait, look at it a little more. So, then what is sacred?

Q: What is sacred? I was going to ask you if there can be a desire that is good?

K: We are not saying good desire or bad. We are examining desire. But the translation of a desire into good and bad depends on the environmental conditioning.

Q: Can we then call it sacred? It is still conditioning to call it anything.

K: Of course, sir, of course. I am sorry, I am not making myself clear. If all the things that thought has created, the technological world as well as the religious world as well as everything, is a material process, then what is sacred, holy?

Q: Sense. Anything without thought.

K: Therefore what is it? Wait sir! I must find out about the ending of thought. I must find out what the limitations are beyond which thought cannot go. That is the real meditation, not all the phony stuff. I have found out what thought is. There must be exploring, investigating, understanding where thought is necessary, where thought has its limitation, where thought realizes its own limitation, so that it does not flow over into something else and create illusions.

So, my son is in this school with these teachers who are conditioned, and the boy is conditioned and the girl is conditioned, and I say, 'Please, help that boy to uncondition himself so that he will live a life without a single conflict'. I have never had a conflict. Forgive me for saying it.

Q: We have had conflict.

K: There is no conflict. If both of us agree to call something a book there is no conflict. But if you insist on calling it a serpent and I call it a book, then there is conflict.

Q: But then what if I say it is a serpent and you say it is a book?

K: Then we do not meet each other.

Q: Right. Then we have a conflict. Do you also have a conflict?

K: No. I see the fact, and I want you, please, if you will kindly, to see the same thing. If you do not see the same thing, what am I to do? If you insist on calling that a serpent, I say, 'Please, touch it', and so on, and you say, 'I refuse', that is the end of it. I am not in conflict with you. Unless you want to prove to me that it is a snake by hitting me on the head.

Q: But if I want to prove to you that it is a snake, would there not be a conflict within you trying to disprove it?

K: No, why should there be? If all of us have agreed to call that a book and you do not, you call it a serpent, it is your conflict, not mine.

Q: Here we may have a conflict. You were saying earlier that desire is sense plus thought.

K: No, it is not what I say, sir. Either it is, or it is not.

Sir, move further. I want to help a student in the school to live a life without conflict. Do you know what happens to human beings then? They flower, they love, something extraordinary takes place in them. I want them to grow up like that; that is my concern, that is my responsibility. And we meet together and say, 'Look, as a teacher living here, it is your responsibility as well as mine'. We must both see the necessity of bringing about an education which will help the student to live a life without a shadow of conflict.

Now, what shall we do? How shall we teach him? Because everything around him is in conflict. His parents are in conflict with each other; the society; everything is in conflict. And I want something so totally different for this child, because I love that child. It is not just love as a sensation, a toy. I love him, I want him to be totally different, not to go through the agony of all the misery of the world. So I will talk. So I say, let us, the parents and the teachers, meet, discuss, see that we are totally responsible, together, that you want that boy to be without conflict. It has never been done, sirs. Do you understand?

Q: Sir, what happens with the parent if the boy says, 'I am not interested. You have talked to me about conditioning, and I see that I am conditioned, and I am first going to make money'?

K: Ah, no. 'Come and stay with us, look at it, live with us, know us, see what is implied'—you discuss with him, take time, trouble. At the end of six months he says, 'Go to hell'. All right, go to hell. Finished. What can I do?

I as the teacher and you as the parent are both concerned with that boy or girl. And we tell that girl, 'Look, do not have a conflict in life, it is not worth it'. We will talk to her—we will put our guts into it, not just talk, but feel for it. And what happens? At the end of a year she says, 'Sorry, I'm not interested'. What are we going to do? You say, 'All right'. But I am not going to leave. I am working at it. If it doesn't succeed with one child, I am going to do something with another.

Q: So you hang in there. It is up to him or her to leave.

K: To come and stay, or leave. What will you do if you have a son who says, 'Sorry, Mum, this is all rubbish you are talking about. You are a square. You are talking nonsense'. What will you do with him?

Q: I will continue to be the way I am.

K: So you say, 'The door is always open. Come in when you want to, leave when you want to'. But I am not going to change the fact for my son, for anybody. Sorry. The fact is that a mind, a human mind must live without conflict; otherwise disaster happens in the world. And my job and my responsibility, my passion, everything is involved in that: to bring that, for a few human beings to do that. I am not looking for success!

Q: That is what we have to be too, right?

K: That is up to you.

Q: Well, that is the way I feel.

Q: You say it has never been done in the world. And yet you have lived without conflict yourself.

K: Yes sir.

Q: So it has been done in the world.

K: (Laughs) Maybe one. I mean, if I have a son, I want him to be that.

Q: Sir, in the experience of a fact, conditioning is so elusive that it can quickly say, 'That is a fact'. And there is that little margin, and you do not know when you are on one side or the other.

K: No sir. Look, you are brought up in America. You know the conditioning of America: money, success, vulgarity, violence, and a marvellous country, and some very nice people. You know all the chicanery of politics. You know everything that is going on around you. And you and your grandparents have created that. That is your conditioning. And if you want to change the world, you have to begin here, which is the world. So if you change, you are bound to affect the world. This is an ordinary fact, sir. You write a very clever, extraordinary book, it affects millions of people.

Q: Wouldn't the commitment to this be a desire? I mean, we do want this. We know what we want.

K: Then let's go for it, let's work for it. It is not desire. The moment it becomes a desire, it will lead us to illusion. Then you become important and I become important. This is important; it is not that I am important because I am carrying that out.

Q: But we know what we want for the child. That is not a desire then.

K: No sir. Our house is on fire. And you put it out. There is not the operation of thought. You move. The world is on fire. Therefore you have to act. You cannot just sit down and say, 'Well, burn'. So you act. If your action is based on an idea, on an authority, then you are contributing to the fire that is going on. But you say, 'This is a fire I must put out. It is my responsibility. I love you'. I love my son, I do not want him to be on fire.

CHAPTER 3.

CAN A HUMAN BEING LIVE WITHOUT CONFLICT?

Krishnamurti (K): May we continue with what we were talking about the last time we met here? We were saying, if I remember rightly, that our social and moral and educational structure breeds a great deal of conflict both outwardly and inwardly. In our dialogue with each other we were saying that education as it is now throughout the world does not altogether eliminate the conflict in man and between men. This is an obvious fact. As we are going to start a school here, is it possible to educate the children—which means of course also to educate ourselves as teachers and parents—to live a life in which every possible conflict is eliminated?

I think that most of us think certain kinds of conflicts are probably necessary, such as competition, the worship of success, conflict of war, conflict in relationship. Apparently, many people accept that conflict does bring something good out of us. But in our discussion and dialogue we were asking whether it is possible at all to be totally free of all conflict, so that the human mind and the brain can function in wider and deeper fields. Because conflict, both inwardly and outwardly, does distort not only relationship but clear thinking. And our society, our culture is based on this conflict. Whether we accept it or not, it is so, practically at all levels of our existence. And where there is conflict, can the human mind develop or change radically in other fields of its capacities?

Our brains and our minds are extraordinarily capable of many things. You must have heard Bronowski and many others who have pointed out what the mind can do and does, both technologically and in its capacity to investigate various fields—biology, architecture, science, and so on. But in our development or ascent we have not eliminated altogether this conflict within ourselves and therefore outwardly. If there were no conflict, then the human mind, human brain could delve very deeply into other fields. So we were discussing whether it is possible for human minds, through education, to transform this energy that is given so much to conflict. That very conflict derives, brings about its own energy. Can that energy be used or function in a different field, at a different depth? As teachers, parents, can we educate the students who come to this school? Is that possible?

I do not know if you have thought about it at all, or merely accepted conflict as inevitable, as part of life, as part of growth. One questions very seriously whether there is a growth based on conflict. You may say all nature is conflict: little trees cannot grow under big trees; little things live on smaller things; and the big beasts live on little beasts. There is an everlasting struggle, effort, right throughout mankind's existence, both in nature and within man. If you are satisfied you say, 'This is inevitable. This is part of the human mind, part of our human existence'. When one accepts it and lives by it, there is very little to be said about it. But when you begin to question it, when you begin to inquire into the whole structure of conflict in which mankind has lived from birth to death, you may ask whether there is not a different way of living.

Education has never gone into this. Religions have said you must live peacefully. They do not mean a word of that, because the priests themselves are in everlasting conflict between themselves and with their neighbours. If one sees the errors or the destructive nature of the conflict, the struggle between man and man and also within oneself, then one can really inquire into whether it is possible for it to end. And if it is possible, how do we educate not only ourselves but also the children in the school? That is the problem.

Please, this is a dialogue, a discussion, an exchange. I do not want to hold the field all the time. It is also your responsibility, because you are the parents.

The society in which we live is degenerating, is totally immoral. If one seriously inquires into this question of conflict, then we are bound to find out, not theoretically but actually, that it is possible to end it. So can a parent, can the educator, can we together bring about a school, a place where children can see this?

I think this is probably a question that was not faced, probably was never even asked of ourselves, of society, of our leaders, and resolved. Probably it has never occurred to us to ask what the quality of a mind is that has had no conflict at all. What we are saying goes totally against all tradition. You may reject a tradition in which you have been brought up, but this is one of the basic traditions among so many others, of which you are unconscious, which you have never questioned. Perhaps in the very questioning, in the very delving into the depth of this problem, one may find the right answer; find a way of living in which there is no conflict whatsoever. Therefore, perhaps we shall know what love means. But we have made love into a terrible conflict.

We have talked to a great many priests about this, to politicians, to some of the cabinet members of governments in different countries. They brush it off. They say, 'This is too utopian, this is not practical. We have to meet the voters who will not even think about all this nonsense'. So everybody pushes this off. I have talked to monks in India and in Europe, monks who are in the church, monks who have left their monasteries, monks who are still in the monasteries, top Jesuits, and some of the top politicians and lawyers. To them, this culture, this society—however efficient, capable it is in certain directions, technologically, industrially—is essentially the product of conflict; which means competition. A painter or a musician who competes with another is not a musician, not a painter. A man who loves painting or music does not compete, it is born out of him.

So can we, as a group of parents and teachers, have a school with children who will understand the process of conflict, the results of conflict, which is the denial of love?

Despite all its benefits socially and economically, will they turn their backs on conflict and live differently?

Some of you are educators. When someone proposes such a thing to you, what is your answer to it? Your serious answer, not just an intellectual, cunning answer. Is it possible to educate children—who are already violent, who are already conditioned by their parents, by their society, by their culture, by their fellow students—to transform them from this everlasting, endless battle? Creation is never competitive, inventiveness is. Human beings have become tremendously inventive, but not creative.

Faced with this problem as parents and teachers, what shall we do? Are you interested in this kind of thing, or do you just call it vague, utopian, and brush it off? I have talked to a great many parents in India and other places who say, 'It is utterly impossible, you are just a dreamer, a utopian, or some kind of nut'. They never face the problem. By condemning one, they think they have solved it. So please do not condemn, please do not brush it off, because it is our problem. As a parent, if you are interested in your children, it is one of the major problems. Learning how to read and write and pass examinations is fairly easy; but if one is really concerned with one's children, one doesn't throw them into a school and forget about them. That is one of the cruel things about a boarding school, if the young children are sent away from parents who wash their hands of them. Here we do not want to do that. What we want to do is have the parents and the teachers responsible for the whole thing. We are building the thing together; it is not that somebody else builds and you send your children to them.

How do you face this question, how do you answer it? You cannot put this question to the children because they will not even understand the issues involved in it. We grown-up people can discuss it intellectually, and actually go into the problem to see the results of conflict, struggle, and whether there is a different way of living altogether.

I wonder if you can go into the question of conflict between what is and what should be. One form of conflict is between what is and the ideal. There is the conflict of the past with the present; the conflict to change what we are into the future, what we should be; the conflict of so-called self-improvement; the conflict in relationship between man and woman, whether sexually or nagging; and the conflict to achieve, to become, to succeed; the conflict of division: black and white; the conflict in ourselves as the observer and the observed. All that is involved, and much more; and, being frightened, we go through endless conflicts to escape from it, suppress it, avoid it, forget it—the whole human psychological machinery, with various levels of our consciousness. Is it at all possible to change that?

If I had a son, what should I do? If you have a son or a daughter, you have lived through endless conflicts: beginning school, college, university—if you are fortunate or unfortunate enough to go to university—conflicts in your business life, in your family, between siblings. If you had a son, how would you educate him, if you do not accept conflict as the inevitable way of life? If you say that it is normal, natural, that it is traditional, that it is essential to survive in society, then there is no problem. It is the same as saying that lying is inevitable, that there is no question about it. But if one begins to question the whole structure, then the question must inevitably arise of how to educate one's children.

Our society has never been able to stop wars. In five thousand historical years, practically every year there has been a war in the world. Imagine how many mothers, sisters, fathers, lovers have wept! And we go on, accepting the tradition. The communists never even question this, and the socialists never even enter into this field to find out. I used to have a great many friends in various fields of politics. They come to a point with this and then say, 'Buzz off, that is enough!'

So we are asking a very fundamental question; and if this school does not solve this problem, then it is not worth it. By the school, we mean the parents, the teachers, all together. You do not say to the teacher or to the school, 'Well, it is your responsibility, solve this problem, we are out of it'. On the contrary, we are saying this is a school where the parents, the teachers, all together are responsible.

Should we discuss first at the verbal, so-called intellectual level, whether it is correct, accurate to ask if a society—whether it is in India, Europe, Asia, or here—that lives on conflict and has so lived for centuries upon centuries, can ever be moral, can ever be truly religious? Religion is not the accepting of all kinds of professional, verbal, theoretical and dogmatic beliefs.

Questioner (Q): At one level I can say yes, this is

something we must do, but at another level I cannot visualize or imagine what lack of conflict would be. And so I don't know.

K: Can you answer what it would be to live without conflict, when one is in the midst of conflict? That would be purely speculative. But the fact is that we do live in conflict, and our children are educated to live in conflict. That is a fact. Can we start with the facts, and see what the results of the facts are in the outward relationship of man to man—whether in the factory, in business, in religion, or in the family—and within oneself? Take the facts, because that is the only way to proceed scientifically and not imaginatively. Is that the way to live? We have accepted it, we have taken it for granted. All religions bless it: 'You will inevitably one day sit next to God—but fight for it'. So taking the facts, proceeding from there, and seeing objectively, not emotionally or romantically, what conflict does in the world, how would you proceed with your children? If, that is, you feel this has to be done, and do not just say, 'Well, sorry, I haven't time'. You have time enough to produce the children.

Q: I am just thinking about conflict. It seems that nations identify themselves or separate themselves through conflict, and cities identify themselves as apart from other cities. If I had a child, I would probably sit and observe that. But the fact is we also separate ourselves with conflict, me against you.

K: Of course. I have been going to a place in Switzerland for the last twenty years. Within a distance of two miles, one village hates the other. If workmen living in one village go to the other, there is trouble. Extend that universally and individually and microscopically. As a mother with children here in the school, knowing you are responsible, not just the teachers, how would you educate them? Practically, not theoretically. If you see the results of conflict objectively, not imaginatively, theoretically, but actually, how would you proceed?

Q: We have children and I find that conflicts in myself that I could overlook before, I can no longer overlook, because I cannot proceed until conflict in myself is resolved.

K: All right. You have conflict in yourself, and you see that your children and other people's children live in conflict. What will you do?

Q: You inquire, first within yourself, to eliminate conflicts.

K: To eliminate conflict. How do you do that? Words have meaning. Sorry. When you say eliminate conflict, that very process of elimination is a part of conflict. No, please, this is much too serious, you cannot play around.

Q: I think you would have to dissect the conflict itself. I think that you have to live with the children on their level, think about the problem back and forth.

K: Do it, please. Here we are, a school. It is not a theory. You are talking theoretically. That is what I am objecting to. You have children. I am asking what you will do.

Q: That is precisely what I would do. I think I would sit with the children and let them discuss it and go through the problem themselves so they can see the end result of it.

K: Can they see it?

Q: I think they can if they are given the chance.

K: How will they see it? When you use the word see, what do you mean?

Q: Understand.

K: All right, what do you mean by the word understand? When you see danger, you move away from the danger. Do you and the children actually see the danger of conflict? Can they see danger as they see a precipice, a snake or whatever? Can you see the danger; you, first, the grown-up people, not the children yet?

Q: You have to deal with it in the moment, as it comes, and I think we have to give up expecting.

K: Madam, we have a school here with children. You are part of that school. What will you do with them? They are violent, undisciplined. (Not that discipline is a marvellous thing; we can go into that.) You all know what American children are. I am not condemning, please, I am just observing. Now, how will you deal with this question of having no conflict? If you see, if you observe that it is essential—see not just the theoretical essentiality of it but actually the utter importance of it, the necessity of it—how will you proceed?

Q: I am saying that we have conflict because we react a

certain way. And when we give up always reacting against everything, conflict is going to go away.

K: Is conflict a reaction? That is what you are saying, more or less.

Q: No, I did not say that. I said that conflict comes from reacting, because we react and we have a conflict.

K: On a very simplistic basis: when one is angry the reaction to that is to try not to be angry. The effort, the conflict is the ordinary process. Now, can you observe anger without bringing the opposite and the dichotomy and all the rest of it, and deal with the anger, not the reaction? I wonder if I'm making myself clear.

Q: You are saying, without identification.

K: Not only identification, but if one is angry, the normal, traditional response is not to be angry, to explain it away, rationalize it, or say, 'I must suppress it', or, 'I was perfectly right to be angry', and so on. And the next time anger comes up, I go on with the same explanation or non-explanation. So the conflict goes on. We are asking whether you can look at anger without the traditional approach.

Q: But that is what I mean by identification: without me looking.

K: Ah, no, I do not want to bring in the "me". Let us stick to this, because that brings in more. Can you observe anger without all the traditional responses? Which is the background that says I must fight it or rationalize it or justify it. Can I teach my student; say, 'Look, don't bring in any explanation. Do not say, "Oh, he hit me, therefore I hit him back. He took my book away," or whatever it is, and get angry'? Can I help him to observe only the fact, not the historicity of the background?

Q: Do you think that would end conflict then? If you were angry, to say, 'Just experience anger, do not bring reasons for being angry'?

K: No, it's much more. Please. One is angry. I am taking that as just a simple example. One is angry, and the educated cultural response is to resist it, to deny it, or to explain it away.

Q: So you would prefer to say, 'I am angry', period.

K: Oh, I could add more. I can add more to it, but that is the ordinary response. We are suggesting that that is the cause of conflict, because the fact is one thing; and the background of all the responses and the explanation is non-fact. Then there is conflict between the fact and non-fact.

Q: Aren't you saying that the conditioning is what causes conflict?

K: It is part of that. Conditioning is part of that conflict. I am a teacher here; I want to educate the children to be totally free of conflict. That means they must be supremely intelligent, not just end conflict. We will go into it. I would say, 'Look, he took your book away, you got angry; and that anger met the tradition which says not to be angry, or not to justify it, and so on. Do not bring in the tradition, just observe the fact'. Here we are. We are educating each other. Sorry, I am not educating you grown-up people, forgive me. You get angry, or jealous or whatever it is, and all the responses of the background of your culture, your desires, your explanations rise up and deny that or try to control the anger. I say to be aware of this rising of the past, but do not let that interfere with the observation of the actual moment of anger.

Q: Then the anger would disappear. You have to have reasons for it, then it will disappear, then it will not be anger anymore.

K: You will find out. It is much more complex than that. You must go into it.

Q: How does one distinguish between observing the fact of anger and all the reasonableness that comes in to support it? The mind can say, 'You're not observing'. It goes back and forth so quickly.

K: Of course, that is part of your conflict. That is part of the conflict.

Q: So conflict is there.

K: No sir. Just take one thing at a time. I am taking anger. If one understands the principle, the truth of it, one has understood the whole structure of it. The fact is I am angry. That is a fact. Because you did something or other. And being a fairly rational being I say, 'Quite right, I am angry; this is why I am angry'. I justify it or do not justify it, and let it disappear. Next time the same thing arises, so I keep on, this battle goes on. And I say, 'It is too stupid to keep up this battle'. I want to find a way of meeting anger without a single conflict.

Now how am I to do it? The moment the tradition meets the present, that is conflict. 'I am the Jew, you are the Arab': it is the same principle. My tradition says I am a Jew, your tradition says Arab. You have taken away something which was mine, and we are at each other's throats. In the same way, there is anger. Can I look at that anger only factually, without any of the interpretations and all the movement of the past interfering with it? Just observe?

Then can I talk to the children and say, 'Look, you are angry'? 'Oh no sir, I am not angry but he made me...' Pin him down and say, 'Look, you are angry', and, 'What happens when you are angry?'

Q: The background comes into the picture now.

K: And he will begin to explain. You go through it. Let him discover it. Because that is part of education. Education is discovery, discovery in freedom, not in you telling him not to be angry. So, to look at anger and not let all the verbal associations with anger come up. The very word anger is a conflict.

Word shapes thought. Language shapes thought. So the word anger is already conditioned. Why does one do this? The child gets angry because you did something or other. What takes place? He has been angry before and he remembers that experience, and associates the present anger with that. He associates himself with that. So he strengthens the past through the present. So anger goes on.

Q: So the memory is what is in there.

K: Yes, the memory, which is the word with all the associations of that word. Then, when you get angry in the present, all that floods in and says you are angry. Now, one has to go very deep. Can the mind realize that words shape thought, that language gives a mould to thought; and that the thought says you are angry, and then all that proceeds? So can I help the child to discover this whole process, so that he says, 'I see. I have an insight into it'? So next time he is angry the responses do not arise, because he has seen it, he has an insight into the momentum of it.

A child has a very delicate brain. He has already been conditioned. He has already been bullied, twisted. To help him, you need a little time, a week or ten days or a month; or, perhaps, if you really understand, you can do it instantly. But with grown-up people it is quite a different matter. They are very deeply entrenched in their tradition. Their tradition is them, and their tradition says that if you are angry, do this, this, and this. For them to see the whole process needs time, because they are so violently entrenched in their position. They reject anything new instantly. So one has to have patience, look at it, talk it over, and so on. But with a child it is quite different because they know instinctively, if it's the proper teacher, that one is trying to do something, helping them; that you are with them, that you are not against them.

Q: But the child has to be willing to give up something that is very comfortable and that they know, for something that they have no knowledge of at all. They have to be willing to give up.

K: Of course. Sir, what do the children need first?

Q: Safety.

K: Security. Complete security; which they do not get at home—forgive me—because the father and mother are too occupied with their own problems, with earning more money, having more of this and more of that. Please, I am not generalizing, I have observed this, watched this for fifty years. It is very difficult for parents to give their time, patience, care to the child. So they send him off to school, hoping that the school will produce something. The child needs complete security. Can the school give that? No school does. But we are saying that unless he has complete security you cannot educate him properly. Security means that the child feels at home with you, trusts you.

Q: But often a child might even be unwilling to give up his own insecurity for security.

K: Therefore you have to deal with it. You have to go into it. So you have to go into why he is insecure—because his parents have neglected him, and so on. You must go very deeply into the whole question of insecurity.

Security is necessary. Security means trust that you really are concerned about him, and not just verbally; that you are really concerned about his health, about his body, how he looks, what he eats, the whole process of it. That is what the school wants. We are going to do this. We are doing it. Otherwise it is not worth it. Also in that security there is a feeling of being protected. Not guided. Being protected means for him to have freedom, and yet know that he is safe.

What would you do if you had a group of students who had been brought up in insecurity, and therefore were violent, distrustful, dishonest, never telling you what they feel? How would you deal with this?

Q: They have to respect you.

K: Why? Why should they respect you? What are you respecting?

Q: Integrity.

K: Ah, no. What are you respecting in a school? The curriculum? The principal? The headmaster? What is a school? The word means leisure. The root meaning of the word school is leisure. To have leisure to learn. So you are respecting learning. And if you are teaching me to learn, I respect you. Because learning is the most sacred thing.

If the student respects learning, then he will also respect the teacher who is teaching him the meaning of learning, the content of learning. Sirs, in the modern world nobody has respect for anybody else. The meaning of respect is to re-consider. It is to re-observe. I re-observe you when you are telling me something. First time I neglect; second time I am diligent in listening to you. That is respect.

Q: There is a problem though, potentially, if the child comes to have this respect for the teacher. If the respect exists, isn't there a tightrope? In other words, the child can easily slip into a kind of hero-worship situation.

K: Ah, no, that is all too silly.

Q: A child would be very susceptible.

K: Sir, as we said, a school is a place of leisure in which learning takes place. That is the meaning of school. That is the dictionary, scholastic meaning of that word: a place of leisure in which learning takes place. Learning not only from books, from the teacher, but learning about oneself, learning about nature. Learning! So learning becomes the most important thing. You are helping me to learn, as a student. I am the student. You are helping me to learn. Therefore I must respect you, because I respect learning.

What we are saying is, if there is no respect for learning, school means nothing, just cultivation of memory, passing exams, getting a job and trotting out into life and making a mess of life. So we are saying a school is a place where you learn, and learning is one of the most sacred things.

Q: But sir, is it sacred to a young child? Does he have any values?

K: No, of course not. The child has no values, but you have to help him, you have to educate him. And you can only educate when you say, 'Look, here you are completely secure'. Unless you feel the importance and the necessity that the child must have complete security, you cannot verbalize it and say, 'You have security'. It means nothing.

One way the child learns is by example. You live a life free of conflict, and the child sees this. Or you live a life in conflict, and the child sees that. To live a life free of conflict, to help the child be free of conflict takes a certain energy, but I do not have that energy to carry it through. For years I have been looking for this theoretical life "free of conflict", but there is not the energy there to make it a fact. Then, you are dealing with a very complex problem of energy. You have energy when you want to do something, don't you? It took energy to come here. Probably you wanted to come here and you did not even think about energy; you said, 'I have to go there because I am interested'.

There are different kinds of energy: energy which is brought about through conflict; a man who wants to be successful has tremendous energy; a man who is aggressive and says, 'I must achieve', is boiling with it. We know that kind of energy very well. When there is the urge of desire for something, there is an outburst of energy. And here is a question: can a mind, human being, live without conflict? You say to live that way needs energy; to find out how to live, expend energy to find out. Now, is there a way of not expending energy to find out, but seeing what conflict actually has done in the world and in oneself? Seeing it, having an insight into it—that very insight is the bursting of energy which pushes conflict away.

I see that conflict is very destructive. Not only in human relationship, which they call love, I see it is tremendously destructive in all relationship. I also see objectively the whole world of division, and I see that where there is division there is conflict and it is very destructive. Objectively and inwardly, I see this actual state going on. I observe it, not trying to rationalize or to justify it. I just observe it. I do not identify myself with one or the other. I say, 'Yes, this is happening'. When you observe without identification, when you observe without the past entering into it, which is the observer, then you have that tremendous energy to wipe it away. You have not tried it!

Q: But mustn't you have a certain level of energy in order to do that, because if your energy is low then all the automatic mind chattering would be there. Therefore you take care of the body and all the other things.

K: Sir, when we talk of energy, one has to go into it from different angles. I was discussing with Dr Bohm about this. I said a mind that is actually nothing—which is not a thing; thing being that which thought has put together—when there is absolutely nothing, emptiness, then there is tremendous energy. He said that is exactly factual; in science emptiness has tremendous energy.

So can the mind, which sees conflict and the wastage of energy in conflict, have a direct insight into it and see the danger of it? When you see something so tremendously, you end it, it is finished. When you see the actual danger of it, it is finished. The seeing is the burning energy.

Q: Sir, one can experience that anger or that frustration or that jealousy and just stop the mind. The mind can quickly say, 'Oh, you are just suppressing'. Is that suppression?

K: No wait, sir. If you smoke, how do you stop it, if you want to stop it?

Q: Well, there are a number of ways to stop the physical act of smoking.

K: Your body is used to nicotine, so it is demanding it and you like it for various reasons. It dulls your mind or something, and you like it. You like the taste of it, and it gives you a sense of companionship with others who are smoking, and so on. Now, how do you stop it, without conflict? Will, exercise of will, is conflict. Right? How do you stop it without conflict? Is there a way of ending it without bringing will into action, which is another form of conflict, without suppressing it, without taking another form of cigarette, all that kind of thing? How do you do it without one single resistance or conflict?

Q: Maybe see the danger of smoking on your health.

K: So, the danger of smoking, but others say there is no danger, old boy, go on smoking. How do you say, 'Well, it is over', without rationalizing? You have never tried these things. Take a habit, any habit that you have. How do you end it without the least resistance, conflict, trouble?

Q: You must see it in its action. You must be absolutely sensitive to the process.

K: Yes. I am in the habit of scratching my head. How do I end it? (Laughs)

Q: Just begin to see the actual, physical movement.

K: Wait sir, half a moment. Take a habit that you have. Find out whether you can stop it instantly without one single resistance or conflict.

Q: I think it's difficult because it took time to develop the habit.

K: So you are saying it took time to develop smoking, now it will take time to end it.

Q: I would say that the mind has to dissect the thought and educate itself.

K: Ah, no, I do not want to go through all that business. I am very clever at examining, analysing, dissecting, but it does not end anything. I want to stop something instantly. Otherwise it is not worth it.

Q: Then you say you won't do it, and that is it.

K: Ah, I do not even say, 'I won't'. That is a form of will.

Q: I stopped smoking. When I really observed what I was doing when I was smoking, really felt what was happening to my body, felt my hand reach for a cigarette, when I really saw the whole thing that I was doing, I did stop. I just stopped, because when I started to do it, I did not want to do it anymore.

K: Instantly, you stopped it? You stopped it like that?

Q: Yes.

K: That is it.

Q: I didn't want to do it.

K: Wait. What does it mean? Being aware of the whole process of smoking, the habits, the various reasons why you smoke; and the fear of smoking, the lungs and so on, you were aware of the total movement physically as well as mentally, aware of the whole structure of a habit. Now, can you stop a habit by being totally aware of it? Any habit. Of course you can.

Q: Because the habit is the lack of awareness.

K: Ah, do not translate it into lack of awareness. Then it becomes, 'How am I to be aware?'

Can one see the mental habits? You saw the physical habits. Can one see the habit of a belief, in which is involved tradition, propaganda, fear, acceptance, obedience; the whole structure and the nature of belief? Or an idea? Can one see an idea or an ideal in which one is soaked inwardly? Can one observe the habit of that totally, and in the very observation, at that very second, it ends?

Q: What is this observation if there is not any thought? What is happening in one's mind, in one's experience of oneself?

K: What is awareness, sir? What is it to be aware? And who is aware? What is the content of awareness? I am aware of this room, the proportions, the colour, the people sitting in it, the various shades of jerseys, and so on. And I am aware of the response to that observation, the like and the dislike, the whole of that. Is that awareness? That is only part of it. What does it mean to be totally, completely aware of a belief, of a conclusion?

Now we have wandered off into something we should not, for the moment.

So can we, as parents and teachers, educate not only what it means to live without control but also to have respect for the art of learning?

CHAPTER 4.

TRANSFORMATION IN THE DEPTH OF HUMAN BEINGS

Krishnamurti (K): This is not an experimental or progressive school as it is understood, progressive in the sense of being a little bit ahead of society. As this is not a progressive or an experimental school, what we intend to do, with your cooperation, with your responsibility, is to educate not in one particular direction, namely cerebrally, but rather to cultivate the whole human mind, the whole being, intellectually, morally, physically, so that the children will meet society totally differently, which means intelligently.

Seeing what is happening in the world, the immorality of the social structure, the chaos, the confusion, the violence, and so on, which you probably know very well, we will help the student, a new generation, to face all that and go beyond it, not accept society as it is. To do that, there must be freedom in the school. By freedom we do not mean irresponsibility, to do what one likes, but the freedom that comes when there is total security for the student, when there is complete trust on the part of the student towards the teacher, and the educator has the sense of total responsibility for the student. This means that there must be security for the child, for the student.

May I go into this question of what it means to be free, what it means to have that discipline which must exist when there is the feeling of complete trust and security? It is generally acknowledged that students must have complete security, which is not given at home—forgive me if I put it bluntly—because the parents are occupied with their own problems, with earning money and so on. So they have no time to give that sense of complete safety, complete sense of wholeness to the child. A school of this kind, if the educator is right, will give a sense of security to the child, that he is at home, but not to do what he likes. The child has come to the school already conditioned by the parents, conditioned by people he lives with. He is already violent, frightened, feeling insecure, and therefore is aggressive. He is already conditioned, shaped by the society in which he lives, by the culture in which he has grown; and to give such a student security means that he will feel that he can do what he likes.

The word discipline means not what is traditionally accepted, but to learn; not to conform, not to imitate, not to comply, not subjugate yourself to a pattern or to an authority, but to learn. Where there is learning there is naturally a responsible adjustment, not compulsive, imitative discipline as it is generally understood. And the word school means a place of leisure in which you learn. That is the real meaning of the word: a place of leisure where one learns. And one cannot learn, in the deeper sense of that word, if there is not a sense of mutual trust and responsibility; you must have that, otherwise you cannot learn. So this is what we are going to do. Otherwise, it is not worth starting a school.

So there must be freedom, security, trust, and the understanding on the part of the parent as well as the educator that we are concerned with the total development of the mind and the heart, with the totality of man, not just one segment of man, as is now being done. So it is your responsibility as well as ours.

We are vegetarians. You might not like that. We have gone into this very deeply, not as a cantankerous, silly thing, some kind of fashion, but nutritionally and scientifically. It is not necessary to eat meat. It is generally being understood by scientists as well as nutritionists that meat is unnecessary, and that the many animals that are killed take up much land. You know all that. It is becoming more and more evident that one can live very healthily, normally, and have plenty of energy by having the right kind of food, which does not mean meat.

That is the basis of the school: that parents understand this and cooperate with the educators here. You are as responsible as the teachers for the school; you do not just send your children and forget them. They come with your consent, with your cooperation, and therefore it is your school too.

That is what we intend—not intend, it is what we are going to do. Intention has very little meaning; whereas the actual fact, the actual activity is that all of us are responsible. If you have money, you help. If you have no money, you give your time. It is our school, we are building it together. So that is the foundation.

Then the problem arises: how are you going to meet a child who is already conditioned? He is already conditioned. He sees parents drink, smoke, use marijuana, drugs, you know, the whole American—forgive me for using the word—vulgarity, which is spreading throughout the world. We come from a tradition in India which has not touched meat for generations, never drank, never smoked, led an astonishingly moral life. All that is going, rapidly! And here in this country there is no tradition at all. It is a very young nation and full of energy.

The problem is that the students, the parents and the teachers, the educators, are already conditioned. Their minds, their brains function on the principle of pleasure. Everything, if you have observed it in yourself and in the world, is based on the principle of enjoyment, having tremendous pleasure. If you can have it; that is called happiness. So our brains are shaped, conditioned to the activity and the pursuit of pleasure. The parents, the child, the educator are conditioned on the principle of reward and punishment. Therefore there is fear. What is the possibility of educating a student not to be afraid, not to be conditioned to the pursuit of pleasure only? Is this possible knowing that most people are conditioned by this? Their religion, their economy, their social relationships, society, everything is based on this principle.

Can the teacher, educator, be concerned with the unconditioning of a student so that he will have intelligence, not pursue pleasure, but will be intelligent? The word intelligence has several meanings. Essentially, it means the capacity to read between the lines; not only in a book but when someone says something. It is intelligence that is going to discover whether it is honest or dishonest. It is intelligence that is going to find out whether a certain activity is worthwhile or not. Is it possible in a school of this kind to uncondition the students so that when they leave they are intelligent, and therefore can meet society intelligently, not accept the patterns of society?

We are all involved in this; it is not that I am laying down something with which you are agreeing. This is your problem, when our whole society, which is so corrupt, immoral, is educating students to be like them. If one sees that, then what is the function of an educator? Is it merely to cultivate the part of the brain that holds memory?

You know, all our education consists, if one observes it in schools, colleges and universities, in gathering information which is called knowledge, and acting skilfully with that knowledge in a corrupt society. Knowledge has become tremendously important. I wonder if you have heard Bronowski talk about the accumulation of knowledge and the democracy of knowledge and the necessity of being tremendously honest with that knowledge, because knowledge is going to change man. We are questioning that. What place has knowledge in the transformation of man and society? Man has apparently lived for millions of years, and fundamentally has not changed. Go to India, go to Japan, go to Europe, come here; we are all the same: greedy, envious, antagonistic, violent, stupid. Mankind has not changed deeply. We may have "pruned the tree" outwardly, but intrinsically, basically, fundamentally, there has not been a transformation of man. And we feel—at least I do feel tremendously—that man must transform himself, otherwise society, the whole thing is going to pieces.

Knowledge is essential, but it is limited and it cannot solve all human problems. Human problems can be solved only when there is the cultivation of the whole of man. The word whole also means sane, healthy, holy. Although man has acquired great knowledge, gone to the moon and so on, that very knowledge may be a hindrance to the transformation of man. As that is so obvious, what can an educator do to uncondition himself, the student and the parent? Because we are all together in the same boat; you are not sitting over on the bank while we paddle; you are as much in the boat as we are. So how can the educator meet a student who is conditioned on the principles of reward and punishment—which means pleasure essentially—and help him to uncondition and live a life which is really intelligent? That is the question, that is the problem. If you have a son, and if you accept that the ordinary progressive, experimental education is still within the field of the cultivation of knowledge, knowing knowledge is not going to solve man's immense, complex problems, then how will you and we meet a student, help him to grow, unconditionally, and therefore be tremendously intelligent?

I hope we are clear about the problem. The teacher is conditioned, the student is conditioned, the parents are conditioned; and we see the importance and the absolute necessity of bringing about a transformation in the psyche of man, which means in the student. Now, what shall we do? If I am a teacher at the school in Ojai, how shall I uncondition myself, the student and, if you are willing, the parent, together? What shall I do?

Will analysis uncondition the student? Will I analyse the teacher and analyse myself, analyse the student? Or is there a totally different way? We have discussed this problem with a great many analysts. Analysis implies the observer and the analysed. But the analyser is the analysed, isn't he? If the analyser is the analysed, then what is he doing? If analysis is merely a continuance of the division between the analyser and the analysed, and therefore a continuance of conflict, then what will we do? Because part of the process of analysis is to uncondition; part of it is to make one different in order that one will accept society.

So what shall we do? If I am a teacher and you are the parent, and both of us are responsible, committed—not just verbally playing tricks with each other but being actually committed, actually involved in seeing the tremendous necessity of bringing about transformation in the psyche, in the very depth of human beings—what shall we do? How shall I as a teacher meet this problem? How will you as a parent meet this problem? Do you say, 'Take my child over. I have my own problems of sex, worries, finance, business; leave me alone, take my child'? Sorry, we are not going to do that. So, we have this problem to face, and we have to face it; the teacher has to face it. The child obviously does not know what we are talking about, poor chap.

How will I, as an educator, meet this problem? First, I see that analysis, however much it is advertised, however popular and partially beneficial it is, has not solved man's problems, has not transformed the human mind. So what shall I do?

We are concerned with the problem of meeting a student who is already conditioned, and the parents are conditioned, the educator is conditioned. How to uncondition the mind so that the child is completely, wholly intelligent—not just partially, in the field of knowledge, which is so small? He is terribly alive, terribly intelligent, terribly cunning there, but the rest is darkness. So, what shall we do?

Q: As I see it, your answer is total security, total involvement, and from total security comes a freedom of inquiry.

K: Yes. So, can we give total security, create the atmosphere, create the feeling, create the sense that the student is at home? 'It is your home. Look after it, care for it and care for your body, care for everything you do!' Can we make that possible? Can we give security of that kind?

Do you know what security means? The student is afraid when he comes, and therefore uncertain, like an animal caught in a cage. He is meeting strangers, feeling lost. How can we give security, help them to feel secure? Which they do not. They do not feel anywhere the sense of being at home, being secure, that people trust them and that they can trust us; that we are looking after them in every direction; that they are cared for physically, morally, intellectually, in every way. You say, 'Well, you can only give such security when there is love'. But the word love is a dangerous word, especially in this country. Is it possible for the teacher, for the educator to have the sense of love?

Love is not pleasure. Love is not desire. Love is not something out of which you are going to get a reward. Love can exist only when there is total abandonment of the self, the "me". We won't go into all that for the moment.

If you, the parent, the teacher, feel that security is the most essential thing, then we have it; you do not have to create it, we have it. If you the parent and I the educator feel the absolute necessity of giving the student the feeling that he is completely secure, we have done it, it is there. This is not something that only the teacher can offer.

While the child is at the school, we are going to give him security; real security, make him feel he is at home. That means looking after his body, his taste, his food, his clothes, the manner of his behaviour, what he thinks, feels, the whole of it. We will give him that for eight hours a day. When he goes home to you, everything is different. Right? So, you are going to destroy that child. We are going to do this on our side, and if you do not do the same thing on your side, the poor chap is going to have a beastly time, isn't he? Obviously. Can we together give this? Can we both see eye to eye about food, about clothes, about behaviour, about the feeling of the whole thing—together—so it is not that when he comes to the school there is one thing, and when he leaves it and goes home there is something different: smoking, drinking, the whole circus? So, if we are doing something but you are not doing the same thing, you are going to destroy that child. It is so obvious, isn't it?

So, it is our responsibility, yours as well as ours, to see that this thing works. Because after all, they are your children. You must love them. I hope you do. See that they have the most marvellous life, not just when they are young people but right through life, and that they do not die, fighting, killing, destroying each other. This is not sentiment, this is not romantic, this is not something utopian, fantastic. We are doing it.

If I were a teacher at this school, knowing the importance of unconditioning the minds of the students and myself, and knowing that introspection or outside analysis is not going to solve the problem of human existence, then I have to meet the student without an analytical inquiry. I will meet him, talk to him, show him the result of a human mind that has lived for a million years and has not changed deeply one iota; and show him what man has created in the world. He may have created the most marvellous technological world, but the rest of it is a rotten world. I will show him all this, talk to him. He will know I am passionate about it by my talk, by my feeling, by my energy, my intensity. He will feel it as you are feeling it now.

So that is what we are going to do. And if you are going to send your children here, you have to understand what we are actually doing, not as an ideal, not as something theoretical, but factual. And therefore you must help us in every direction.

Full stop, I have finished. Can we now have a dialogue about it?

Q: I would like to be clear in my mind about the concept of the problem of conditioning. You just said that you would talk to him about it, and that he will feel by our intensity what we are saying. There is the passion, but is this talking unconditioning the mind?

K: I would talk to the student and also teach him in class. When I am teaching mathematics or history or whatever it is, I would talk about what the world is, not just talk to him on a walk, I would be at it all day.

Q: But what I am trying to ask is: isn't that another form of conditioning? What is the difference? That is what I do not understand.

K: Oh, no. I will show it to you. I can be a Catholic and become a Protestant, but it is the same darkness. Sorry. Or become a Hindu or go to Zen, or this or that. But we are talking of unconditioning the mind, not reconditioning in a new form.

Q: I understand what you are saying, but I still do not understand how you really accomplish that.

K: Look, freedom does not imply freedom to go from one thing to something else, freedom from being a Hindu to become a Catholic. That is generally called freedom, freedom of choice. Please, this is very important. We think we are free when we can choose. Choice in itself indicates lack of freedom. When do I choose? When I am confused. Of course. When I am clear, I do not choose. When I am clear that all religions, whether Hinduism, this, that or the other, are organised propagandist processes, I will not jump from one fire to another fire. It is finished. Please, I know what I am talking about, because I was the head of a big organisation. (Laughter)

Q: So is the Pope though. What is the difference between the organisations? Because what you have is still an organisation.

K: Oh no, this organisation is merely to publish books, to start a school. It has nothing to do with religion. This is merely to start a school, to see that the books are published, to see that the speaker has a place to talk. That is all. There is no church, there is no conversion, there is no proselytising, there is no head, chief.

Q: In the educational process that you are delineating, isn't it necessary that the teachers themselves first be de-conditioned?

K: Ah, look what that means: first I must be unconditioned, then I can begin with the problem of unconditioning.

Q: Yes.

K: But no teacher is unconditioned. Therefore what takes place? While talking about unconditioning with the student, he is himself unconditioning. He is aware of his conditioning.

Q: By talking about it?

K: By talking about it, being in contact, seeing the importance of unconditioning.

Q: That is what is done in psychoanalysis as well, which is something that you have criticised.

K: Ah, no, no. We must go into analysis very deeply because it is quite a different problem. What is implied in analysis? First, the analyser and the analysed. A time, interval, a gap from now, till, say, a year from now. In that time interval there are other factors entering, other factors which will condition him.

Q: I understand that. What I do not understand is how the analogy of psychoanalysis is in any way different than the analogy of the teacher and the student.

K: Quite right, sir. Your question is legitimate. Let's go into it. I have a student and I realise that I am conditioned and he is conditioned. That is a fact. Now, how shall I deal with the problem when I see that analysis is not going to solve it? I see it; not verbally, I have an insight into it. I see that is not worthwhile. So my whole mentality is different. Suppose one thinks analysis is the way, and you see it is not the way. Then you have completely turned away from it. Therefore what has happened to your mind? You are no longer analysing. You are free of that process. Your mind is then fresher, non-traditional, non-accepting of the authority of Freud, this or that. So your mind is much freer to look. Right?

Q: Yes, I do understand that.

K: No, no, you are doing it, not understanding it.

Q: (Laughs) All right.

K: If I am the teacher and you are the student, you and

I are both actually involved in this. You are no longer analysing and I am no longer analysing. Both of us have turned away from it.

Q: If in fact we have.

K: Ah, that is the problem. You are conditioned. You say, 'My dear chap, you are also conditioned against analysis'. You are conditioned to accept analysis, and suppose I am conditioned not to accept it. We do not meet at all. But if we are both inquiring, not verbally but actually, then our inquiry demands that we both be free to look at the whole process of analysis. Look! Not conclude an opinion, not come to an agreement, but both together see the actual fact. Then what takes place between us? What does it mean when you and I are both free of a certain tradition—we will use that word—both of us free of a certain fact which we have accepted, with which we have lived? We discard it, what happens to our minds?

Q: They become clear.

K: Clear. That is all. You are already unconditioned.

Q: I understood what you were saying about intuition, if that is the word you used.

K: No, I would rather use insight. It is a better word than romantic intuition that can mean all kinds of things.

Q: I can understand in an intellectual way that such deconditioning is what I am striving for. It is bridging the gap between intellectual understanding and the actual insight which effects the transformation in myself. Is there a way that is done or not done?

K: I understand, sir. There is no way. Right? There is no system, because if there is a system, a method, then that becomes another conditioning. So you discard systems. Analysis is part of a system. So both of us see or have an insight that any system, any conclusion which is a system, does not bridge the gap. So what will? If analysis, a conclusion, an idea will not bridge this, then is there anything to bridge it? What divides? Analysis, ideas, conclusions, opinions. If you do not have that, there is no gap to bridge.

Sir, let's come back. I am the teacher and there is the student. I see the importance of unconditioning myself as well as the student. It is not an intellectual conclusion, not a conclusion which I have derived through the observation of history and come to a conclusion. That is still intellectual and, therefore, divisive. I see the fact that conditioning as a Hindu, Muslim, communist is very destructive. It is destroying mankind. That is a fact. Therefore I have no divisive instincts, divisive opinions, conclusions. I am going to convey this to the child. That is my job, it is my responsibility, it is my affection, it is my care. I am involved in it totally. I am going to see this is done, that he has no divisive feeling in him. I will talk to him in the school, and when I teach history I will point out how everything is war, violence, division, personal corruption, personal ambition. I will point it out day after day. Of course. If I am intense, he will understand in a week's time.

So, I would talk to my students and say, 'Look, do not come to any conclusion about anything. Find out, inquire, go into it, but not with a prejudice, with a fixed point of view, because then you are blocking yourself. To inquire you must be free'. A good, first-class scientist does not start with a conclusion; he inquires, moves, and discovers.

Q: Does he come to a conclusion?

K: When he comes to a conclusion, he is no longer a scientist.

Q: Excuse me, sir. Would that movement of inquiry be from the state of not knowing?

K: Yes sir. You see human beings conditioned by their religion. A whole group in India call themselves Hindus; there are Jews, Arabs, communists, socialists, the English, the Germans, the French. There is this divisive process; which means eternal conflict. Which is what is happening: in India, the Muslim against the Hindu and the Hindu against the Muslim; the Arab and the Jew; all through the world. I ask why we should live that way. I know it is the accepted tradition, that you are educated that way, but why should we live that way? There may be a different way of living. Let's find out. Let's sit together and find out. Find out how to educate our children totally differently.

Q: Mr Krishnamurti, I came here from New Mexico for the express purpose of seeing if there was an environment where my 10 year-old son can be free to inquire. If you are here or people who feel as you do are here, not using the words, not imitating you, none of that stuff, but who feel as you feel and who have taken the time and care, it is possible.

K: It has been my responsibility to the people who are

here to see that this happens. We meet, we discuss, we go at it. It is not that I just talk and disappear. I spend a month in each place. I will spend three months in this place. It is not just something new that I am starting, I have been at it for fifty years and more. We will create it. There are people here who say, 'Right, we will do it together, create the school'.

Q: You were saying that when the child leaves the school and goes home, the parent should not be in conflict with what is going on at the school. Of course there are problems and we are conditioned in our ways, and we may find that we like some of our conditioning.

K: So, for your child, will you give up something which is pleasurable? Nobody will. And that is what we are demanding.

Q: But of course we will, of course we do. This leads me to my next point. When the child finishes what is termed the time of education, that child has to go out into this world of conditioning and everything else out there; and has, in some way, to accept that world or deal in some way with that world. Isn't there anything beneficial in finding something different in the home?

K: Maybe. But the child may consider something to be wrong at home. How will you meet him? He may come home from us and feel that something is wrong at home. He is frightened to tell you, or he may tell you. Will you change, or will you say, 'Now, sit down, let's inquire'? 'Let's inquire, let's go into it'; not convince him that you are right, that we are wrong, or we are right. Together, sir, together you and we are educating ourselves and the child.

Q: That is what I would say, but if you are eating meat at home and the school is vegetarian, well you can explain that perhaps.

K: Of course. He will say, 'Mummy, you eat meat, let me be vegetarian'. That is what is happening. If the food we give is first-class, which it is going to be, then he will go home and say, 'Please, you eat meat, give me vegetarian'. But if you say, 'No, old boy, you're going to eat meat', it is opinion against opinion, and so on. Oh, this is just common sense. We get into habits, and then we find those habits so pleasurable that we hate to give them up. We are saying to the child, 'Do not get into habits—smoking, drinking, sex, thinking in one direction'. Sir, be a river that is flowing!

If I were a student and you were my parent, and I have been through the regular system, what happens? I go my way and you go your way. We meet on birthdays or something or other, and we separate. I live my life and you live your life. We are saying that is totally wrong. You are my father, you have to look after me, there is a relationship.

Q: Children will still tend to imitate. Children will still desire to eat meat when they see other children eating meat.

K: Of course, sir. That is part of the same difficulty; children want to imitate, belong to something, belong to a group, because they feel belonging to a group gives some security. If I lived in Italy and did not belong to the Catholic world, I would feel left out. So I join it for financial purposes, emotional, and so on. So we are all inclined to imitate, conform. That denies freedom.

So, sirs and ladies, we will discuss in detail together what we can do. We are together in this, with this problem. It is your problem as well as ours.

One would rather begin sanely and rationally with a little. Not these grand affairs. There is beauty in the little.

CHAPTER 5.

IS MY RELATIONSHIP TO MY STUDENT A CONCEPTUAL ONE?

Krishnamurti (K): We were talking over together how to help the student, the educator and the parent to transform themselves totally, to uncondition the mind without analysis if that is at all possible. If we could go into that a little more deeply, perhaps it might be worthwhile.

The other day on television, was shown a series of events throughout the world—in Japan, in China, in Africa, in India—about the total confusion of each nation arming itself at the expense of other nations. This implies a mind that has been conditioned to think in terms of its own security at the expense of the totality of other human beings. Any intelligent, fairly decent-minded human being must inevitably ask whether it is at all possible to have a different kind of society, a different kind of human being. Is it possible to uncondition the mind? If analysis is not the way—and I am not sure you would agree to that—then what is? What is one to do? That is the question, isn't it? If analysis—that is, examination of the cause, effect, and the effect becoming the cause, the whole chain of causation, which is the accepted, traditional thing—is not the way, then how is one to approach unconditioning the mind?

If one is an educator or a parent, as some of us are, that would be our problem. What shall we do both in the class and outside the classrooms, without analysis, not only to help ourselves to uncondition, but also, in relationship with the students, to uncondition them? If you have thought any more about this question, perhaps we could discuss it further.

In the whole of Western civilization, through Freud, Jung and all the others, a new tradition has been established of introspective and professional analysis. In India also this is an old tradition. That is, examine the origin of the mischief—whether you were put on the pot rightly or wrongly as a baby—and work from there. We are asking quite a different thing. Is it at all possible, without this self-critical or professional analysis, for the mind to be unconditioned?

Questioner (Q): One of my own difficulties in inquiring into this is a lack of real clarity regarding simply what conditioning is.

K: What is conditioning? Your mind, sir, one's mind, the human mind, is the result of centuries of experience.

Q: As I see it, my mind is the result only of my own experience since I have been born, which is not centuries. I do not understand what you mean by centuries of experience.

K: One's brain is the result of time, isn't it?

Q: Only the time since it has been born.

K: It is time in the sense of growth, accumulation of experience, knowledge, and the brain cells containing this knowledge and functioning through the response of thought in daily life. Over many, many years, centuries of accumulation have been passed on, generation to generation, through heredity and social changes, economic pressures, religious or scientific beliefs. All that is the conditioning of a brain, of a mind.

Q: Is the conditioning then belief?

K: Belief, ideal, accepting conflict as necessary.

Q: All of these are forms of belief, are they not?

K: Not only belief but they are an actuality, the conflict between human beings, man, woman, in their relationships. There has always been conflict, and pursuing, living in conflict is part of conditioning. Suppose one is brought up as a Catholic; one has all the paraphernalia of rituals, accepting authority, accepting Jesus Christ as the only saviour, son of God, the Virgin Mary, ascending to heaven physically. These are all dogmas asserted by the Church and accepted through two thousand years, as an actuality.

Q: Accepted as an actuality. Which means belief.

K: Accepted belief. They go beyond that, beyond belief, saying, 'It is so'. In India it is also the same old thing in a different form. It is not only a belief; to the believer it is an actuality.

Q: To every believer his belief is an actuality?

K: Of course. If I do not believe I say, 'What rot all this is!' The believer goes to Mass, and so on, and lives the belief as actuality, which is propaganda, which is the conditioning, which is the constant repetition that Jesus is the only saviour. He accepts it, and that acceptance is based not only on convenience and economic pressures and so on, it is a two thousand year old tradition. In India there is a five thousand year old tradition of castes. There is the nationalistic tradition: that you are an Englishman, German, Russian; that if you are born in the communist world, there is no God, there is only the state. These are all forms of conditioning.

Q: But is this thing which we are trying to impart here, this thing which we are trying to enable the student to see, not another form of conditioning?

K: It all depends on how you do it. Suppose you are my student. I am aware that I am conditioned as an American, with all the American ideas, ideologies, vulgarities, sensualities and the sense of freedom, permissiveness; the whole gamut of the modern American society: money, success, pleasure, do what you want, and so on. If I am an American, I have been conditioned to that. You are a student coming to the school conditioned, violent and if your parents are divorced, disturbed. So you come conditioned and I come conditioned. Conditioned in the sense that the culture in which I have lived has shaped my thinking through school, college, university. And you have come that way too. So the student and the educator both come conditioned to pleasure and pain. That is a fact. We are asking how an educator is to uncondition himself and the student without the process of analysis.

Q: It would seem that in order to do that we need to see with clarity what conditioning is and also what conditioning is not.

K: How do you know what is not conditioning if your mind is conditioned? That is just an idea projected from a conditioned mind. We know exactly what we mean by that. If I am conditioned, how can I see what an unconditioned mind is, except as an idea, as an image of that word as an ideal?

Q: I did not mean that. I meant facts, very ordinary facts. It is daylight right now. I mean there is a perception of facts at a certain level which is not the result of conditioning. One can perceive if it is snowing outside. That doesn't mean that I believe it is snowing. It is snowing and I see it. So that is not a conditioned reaction.

K: Yes. So do you recognize as a fact, not as an idea, that you are conditioned? Not because somebody tells you, not because you have read about it or, in talking it over, realized that you are conditioned. Is it a fact or an idea? If I am the educator, do I see "I have been conditioned" as an idea, as something which is non-fact? Idea is non-fact. No?

Q: Is it necessarily so?

K: Oh, isn't it? The word idea, as we were saying the other

day, comes from the Greek, which means seeing. The root meaning of that word is seeing, not what we have made of it. We see and then make an abstraction of what we see, which is an idea. It is very simple. I say to you, 'You are conditioned'. You listen to the statement. From that statement you draw an abstraction, which is the idea, and with that idea you examine whether you are conditioned. I wonder if you see the thing actually, not as an idea? This is simple.

Q: There is the fact of actuality, and there is the supposed fact of belief.

K: Oh, the moment you suppose, it is not a fact.

Q: But isn't our difficulty that some perceptions are non-fact, and we do not see them that way; we see them as facts?

K: That is what I want to come to. We said just now that you are the student and I am the educator. We both are conditioned. Now, do I see the actuality of conditioning, the actual conditioning, or is it an idea?

Q: It is an idea.

K: Ah, I want to find out. Is it an idea or an actuality with you?

Q: It is an idea.

K: Ah, no. Why?

Q: Because if I were to see it…

K: Ah, no, not if. Why? Why is it an idea?

Q: I do not know why, it just is.

K: Ah, no sir, it is very simple. Go into it, you will see it.

Q: It seems that at certain times it is seen as a fact and at other times it is seen as an idea.

K: No, a fact is always a fact, you cannot change it into an idea. Look sir, is a poisonous snake an idea?

Q: On one level, I make it an idea.

K: You see a poisonous snake, a rattler. The seeing is not an idea. That is a fact. From the seeing you draw a conclusion that it is dangerous, and you do something about it.

Q: If you know it is dangerous. If you do not know it is dangerous, sir, then…

K: Ah, then of course you play with it and get stung. But when you have seen the danger of a precipice, you move away from it.

You are moving away from the central issue, if you don't mind. I am the educator, you are the student. We both are conditioned. Now, when I say that, do you see it as an actuality or a concept? This must be established first, before we go any further.

Q: It is a concept.

K: It is a concept. Why?

Q: We do not see it.

K: No, please, just listen to my question. Why do you make it into a concept?

Q: Because if you saw it as a fact, it would no longer be there.

K: We will come to that point next. First I am asking why we live in concepts or form concepts.

Q: Is it not part of our habit?

K: Go into it, sir, a little bit more. Do you make pain into a concept?

Q: Probably. I think to an extent I do, because I let it intensify.

K: No, wait, just listen. I have a toothache. Do I make a concept of it?

Q: No, that is a feeling.

K: Wait sir, do go into it a little bit, do not answer me. Please find out for yourself and see. You have a toothache. The pain is actual. You go to the dentist and so on. There is no concept.

Q: But if you think about the pain...

K: No, wait sir. First see. First see. We will go step by step into this if you do not mind. Go slowly into this. We are asking why the human mind lives in concepts and creates concepts; the word concept: to conceive. Why does the mind do it? If I hear a statement like—what? Make a statement.

Q: Sunsets are pretty.

K: Sunsets are beautiful. I make a statement of that kind to communicate with you. I see the sunset and it is very beautiful, the colours, the radiance, and so on. You are there, and I say, 'How beautiful that is!' That is only to communicate verbally a feeling which I have. There is no concept, is there?

Q: Yes there is. The concept is that you conceive beauty. The other night we were driving home with someone who said, 'The sunset is beautiful'. The lady with us said, 'Don't you know that red in the sky is caused by pollution? I think it's grotesque'. Consequently, there was a conception on both sides. There was the conception of the beauty in the eye of the beholder, and the grotesquery in the eye of the other lady.

K: Sir, look, we asked what a concept is. To conceive. That is, to think. To conceive something is to think about something.

Q: To create an abstraction, basically.

K: That's it. Why does the mind make an abstraction? When you see something, why does thought say, 'It is beautiful', and make a concept of it, and then want the pleasure of that sunset the next day? I see the sunset and make an image through thought of how beautiful it is. Or you say, 'No, it is not beautiful'. So you make an image, a concept, and live in that concept. Why does the mind do this?

Q: One reason that it creates concepts is to classify information.

K: The sunset has gone but I still have the concept, I still have the picture, the image; the verbal structure of it still remains. The actuality is finished but the verbal picture remains. Why? When the sun is down and it is dark—finished with it. Why does the mind make a structure of it?

Q: To derive joy, pleasure, whatever you want to call it, satisfaction.

K: That is not creation. Concepts are not creation.

Q: To conceive is to create.

K: So now we must go into the word create. What is creation and what is inventiveness? We must go into this question slowly, if you don't mind. Why does the human mind not only make concepts, verbal structures, pictures, but live in them, and does not see the actual and finish with it?

Q: I think it gives the mind a sense of stability and power to be able to order and classify its experience. It is afraid to live in unknowns.

K: You are guessing. Look, I am not good—"good" in quotation marks. Let's not discuss your opinion and my opinion of good, but say, 'I am not good'. And I make an idea that I must be good. The idea that I must be good is a concept and therefore not real. The fact is that I am not good, I am not kind. Whatever it is, I am not. But I make a concept of it and say I must be good. Now, why do we do this? Is it part of our culture?

Q: It is part of conditioning.

K: I do not want to come back to that word conditioning. Culture, tradition, our education, all our religious structures say, 'You are not this but you must be that'. So I am asking: is it part of our social, environmental propaganda that makes us live in the future, the ideal, and not here? We never say, 'This is so'. Writers and intellectual people and religious people give tremendous importance to ideals. 'He is an ideal boy, he has ideals', which is future. Why does the mind do this? Please listen. Is it because it does not know how to deal with the present?

Q: Maybe it fears the present.

K: No, no, do not introduce the word fear. Stick to one thing. I am asking if it is because it does not know what to do with the present, and therefore it conceives a picture of what it must be doing, and escapes to that? Is it because it does not know what to do with what is?

Q: Well, why doesn't it?

K: Wait! First grasp that. First see that.

Q: Or it goes back to the past.

K: Either live in the past or in the future. I live in the past and control the present through the past. Obviously. Or I live in the future because I do not know what to do with the present. So ideals, concepts are escapes from the present. Is that an idea or actual?

Q: Idea.

K: One has made a statement that we live in the future, the

ideal, the goal, the "should be", because we do not know how to deal with the present. Therefore that is an escape. Now, is that statement a concept or an actuality? If it is an actuality, there is no escape. Right? If it is not actual, you are off into some other field. So, I have a problem. I am the educator, you are the student. I know as a fact, not as an idea or concept, that I am conditioned, or that I am an Indian, with all their superstitions, with all their ideas, with their beliefs, and so on. Or, I lived in England for many years, and I am conditioned by that. I know it, I see it, and not as an idea.

If I am an educator in a school of this kind, and I realize I am conditioned, is the realization a conceptual realization or is it an actual realization as when I have a toothache? Because that makes a tremendous difference. If I am living in a theory, in a speculative, conceptual world of conditioning, then my relationship to you is conceptual, not actual. Look! If I say I love you, is it a concept?

Q: Obviously love is not a concept.

K: How do you know? See what you are saying: 'Obviously love is not a concept'. Is that so? I am just asking. I hold your hand. Is that a concept?

Q: No.

K: No. But from holding your hand I draw a concept: how nice it is, how pleasurable it is, how I would like to hold his hand further. All that is non-real. Holding hands is an actual fact. Now, do you see, are you aware as an actual fact that you are conditioned? If you do not, you are playing with words. But if you see it as an actual fact, then my relationship to you as an educator is entirely different, because then I am dealing only with facts, not with concepts.

Q: Sir, would it matter that I can look at my behaviour and become aware of a certain pattern of my behaviour being habitual, being a conditioned pattern of behaviour? Does that mean I am aware of only a part of my conditioning or of the totality?

K: Good enough. Begin with that. You are saying you are aware, know or see actually the pattern of your behaviour. A later question is: can I see the whole structure of behaviour? That is the question you are asking, isn't it? Can I see not just part but the whole behavioural structure, the nature of behaviour, how it happens, and so on? Can I see the whole of behaviour or only part?

Q: But usually I can see only a part.

K: Therefore leave it there.

So, I am asking: if I am the educator, is my relationship to my student a conceptual relationship? That is, "I am conditioned" is an idea, and you also are conditioned as an idea, so our relationship is at a level of non-fact. Stick to that. Until you see that, we will not move. Bring it a little closer. If I am married, if I have a wife, is my wife a concept?

Q: No, she is a fact.

K: Ah, wait sir, go slowly. It is much more complex than

that. We made it a picture, a concept, an image, a structure. If I have a wife, is my relationship conceptual? Is it a series of pleasurable or painful incidents which have built a structure which I call a concept, a picture, an image? I am asking those who are married or about to marry, who have a girlfriend or a boyfriend, if your relationship is conceptual. You are stuck, aren't you? (Laughter) Not being married, I can say most people's marriages are conceptual.

Q: It can be nothing else.

K: That is all. Keep to reality. If my relationship to my wife is conceptual, which is so, then what does it mean?

Q: But it cannot be that way, because everything is changing every minute. How can you live by a concept?

K: Everything changes every minute, but change is in the conceptual field. I have built a picture of my wife—conceptual. She changes. I change the concept a little bit, but it is still within the field of concepts. This is so obvious, I do not know why we are fighting it. What is the relationship of human beings, man, woman, when it is on the level of concepts?

Q: There is none.

K: I have had pleasure from my wife, sexual and other forms, and that is the picture I have. And if I live in a conceptual world, as 99.9 per cent of people do, what happens? When I live with somebody in a world of non-actuality, non-factuality, what is my relationship? I have no relationship.

When I realize that I am not living in a conceptual world but dealing with the actual conditioning, my relationship to the student is entirely different. That is my point. You see, what has happened is that we have cultivated the intellect enormously; and the function of the intellect is to think clearly and form pictures clearly. Move intellect a little bit away from that and it does not know what you are talking about. All our education is to cultivate memory, to cultivate the capacity to think in terms of knowledge, memory. Isn't it the whole function of the intellect to reason, to think, to draw a conclusion, and act according to that conclusion, which is a fiction, which is a concept? I think one thing, do something else. When I am dealing only with fact, what takes place? There is no contradiction.

Sirs, when I have a concept, an idea, an ideal, totally different from the actual, then there is conflict. If I as an educator actually see that I am conditioned, not as an idea or concept, then my relationship to the student is wholly different. I am dealing with facts so I can go into that with the student and work out the conceptual business and push it out. We can find out how to live together, educate each other, only with facts.

Q: By concepts do you mean expectations?

K: Yes, a concept is an expectation, accepting authority, saying, 'I am much better than you are'; putting myself as an educator on a pedestal and doling out information.

Q: Does dealing with something as a fact mean I only deal with something on a perceptual level, without thought?

K: Ah, wait, no, it is much more complex, sir. Can you perceive something without thought? This leads into all kinds of problems.

Sir, as we were saying some time ago, there is the art of listening. The art of listening means I listen to put what you are saying in its right place. Art implies putting everything, everything, in the proper place. That is the meaning of that word. So when I listen, am I listening to the statement or making an abstraction of that statement into a concept and trying to reason with that concept? If so, my concept is different from your concept. You and I have different opinions. You say, 'Yes, it is an ugly world'. That is your opinion. I say, 'It is a beautiful world'. That is an opinion. But if we are dealing with facts, there is no opinion. If I am a liar, that is a fact. I am a liar. I can do something about it; but if I say, 'Well, I must not lie', 'This is the reason I lied', 'It is good to lie', then I am off.

So, as an educator, my relationship to the student becomes entirely different when there is no concept at all. Can you as an educator do this? Sir, as an educator I would hold a student's hand. Then my relationship, which is non-conceptual, is different, isn't it? Actually.

Q: Yes.

K: But when I am not holding your hand, I have made a series of pictures, conclusions, concepts, and from that concept I hold your hand, isn't there a difference?

Q: Of course.

K: So, when you as an educator are dealing with the student, you see you are both conditioned. When you are dealing with abstraction, a conclusion, our relationship is entirely different from when it is an actual thing to you.

Q: Can I ask, in a non-conceptual way, if you hold my hand, why do you hold my hand?

K: I have told you, sir. I love you, therefore I hold your hand.

We must come back. We asked how, as an educator I am to deal with concepts, knowing that I am conditioned and that my students are conditioned. That is the central question we are asking. If I am dealing with concepts then there is no ending of conditioning. I can talk endlessly; it is your opinion, my opinion; Bertrand Russell says yes and the Pope says no. You can play that game endlessly. But when I see the actual, my relationship to the student is entirely different. It is the function of the teacher to establish that we are dealing with facts and not with suppositions, ideals, concepts. You are conditioned to live in ideals, concepts, and somebody like me comes along and says deal with facts, then you can do something. I can imagine myself flying a jet, but actually to fly it, I have to work, I have to study, I have to practise. If you are the educator and I am the student, knowing that we both are conditioned, we must realize it factually, not theoretically. That means no concept.

You see, that is your conditioning. That is the difficulty. Somebody comes along with something new and I am so conditioned that I say, 'I cannot see what are you talking about. Show it to me'. He shows it, but you cannot see it because you are so heavily conditioned. It is a habit. It is your tradition. It is your way of living, and it becomes terribly difficult to break all that and say, 'All right, let me deal only with facts'.

Q: Is it impossible to describe the actual nature of the relationship?

K: Suppose I am unconditioned. I see the fact, not a concept, not a picture, not in imagination, not that somebody told me, and so on. I actually see the fact that I am conditioned; and I know, as an actual fact, the student. My relationship to the student is non-conceptual, but the student's relationship to me is conceptual. So I have to deal with this problem. His is conceptual, mine is not. So we are living at different levels. How am I to meet that student or help him? How am I to meet him when he lives there and I live here? How am I to bring these two together? I am living with facts; no concepts, no ideals, no goal, no future. I am dealing only with the fact of what is, which is that I am conditioned and that he is conditioned. Then what shall I do? What takes place between us? Can there be a relationship between a man who lives in concepts and a man who does not live in concepts? Between a person who actually lives in facts and one who does not, what is their relationship? Non-factual, obviously. But you are my educator. What will you do?

Q: Discuss, which is what you are doing now.

K: With a student you can a little bit. But he is likely to say, 'Sorry, I will go on with my concepts'. This is what is actually taking place now.

Q: As far as one can make out, one does live in fact. But

you come along and say, 'You cannot tell the difference between fact and non-fact'.

K: I do not say it. No, I never said that.

Q: Well, that's reading between the lines a little bit, sir.

K: No, no, do not read between the lines.

Q: Is that not the implication? If one is conditioned and one does not see one's conditioning, then that is the same as not being able to distinguish between the fact and the non-fact.

K: Sir, let's keep it very simple. You are an American. You have been educated here. You have all kinds of ideas. Be simple about it. No?

Q: I have some ideas, yes.

K: Ideas, conclusions, opinions, judgments. You have been brought up as an American, and I am just a beginner. I already have my own conclusions, my own prejudices. Then what is our relationship? You are conditioned, I am conditioned. What is our relationship? We live on the same floor of conclusions of tradition, of non-tradition, of vulgarity, of violence. We live on the same floor. Now, if you see the actual fact of conditioning and I do not, if we are not on the same floor, what is our relationship?

Q: Not meeting.

K: Not meeting. Now, how will we meet?

Q: One or the other reaches out.

K: Conceptual reaching. I am here, and you are over there. So I am asking: what shall I do as an educator to bring us together, in harmony, so all live on the same floor? What shall I do?

Q: Could we say that you continue to live in your clarity and, in a sense, not do anything?

K: No, no, do not theorize, sir.

Q: What would you do?

K: If I tell you, then you will begin to discuss it as an idea, as a conclusion. I am asking you. What will you do under these circumstances, sir? Not what would I do.

Q: Be quiet with it, sir?

Q: Deal with the fact of the conditioning.

K: But I do not know what the fact is.

Q: Oh, I thought that the educator understood that the fact was there.

K: Sir, he is conditioned, I am conditioned. We both are conditioned, the student and the educator. Then the matter is very simple. I strengthen my conditioning or weaken my conditioning; I help him to strengthen his conditioning or to weaken it. That is all. That is very simple.

But then I see the actuality of my conditioning, the actual fact, not a theory, not a concept. I see that I am an Indian with all that blasted stupidity, or a communist with all that stupidity. I see it. I am that. I am that, and therefore

I am dealing only with fact. He is my student and he does not know how to deal with facts. He lives in concepts. How am I to deal with this chap? The question is simple, isn't it? How am I, who does not live in concepts, to deal with one who lives in concepts? Which is what actually is going on now. What shall I do? Throw up my hands and give up? What shall I do? How shall I get into contact with that boy, with that girl, with you who live in there when I do not live there? What shall I do to bring a communication with each other?

Q: Can I show the other that he or she lives in concepts?

K: Just go into it. Just listen carefully. I want to show it to you. Please, sir, make it actual. I want to show you a picture, a painting. Which means what? I must persuade you, I must talk to you. That means you must be willing to see. Right? Willing to see the picture which I have painted; not say, 'Oh, you are a rather bad painter', or a good painter, or 'You have a name'. I just say, 'Please, sir, do look at this picture'. That means you must be willing to look. Right?

Q: And you must also be willing to share.

K: You see, you are bringing in something else. I am sharing. Do not bring in "willing to share". I am showing it to you. First, the student must be willing to listen.

Q: Of course. Obviously.

K: Obviously. Now, how will you make him listen? Not persuade him, not twist his arm, not reward him or punish him. How will you make him listen to what you have to say? Are you listening to what I have to say? How are you going to help him to listen to what you are saying?

Q: By being with him and not making an effort, simply by doing it.

K: Will you? Are you doing it now?

Q: No, because I am explaining it.

K: Ah, no, are you listening or are you saying, 'This is so, this is so'?

Q: I am thinking.

K: Yes. So you are not listening. So how am I going to persuade you to listen? With reward, punishment because you are conditioned to reward and punishment? That is the only thing we know. So if we discard those two, will you listen to me?

Q: If you were very personally interested in the student...

K: I am not personally interested. I want him to listen to the birds! He should listen to the birds. He should listen to music. He should listen to somebody saying something. Listen! Do we ever listen? Are you listening to me?

Q: I think we listen sometimes.

K: Do you listen to the statement? Listen, not, 'No', 'Yes', 'It's right, wrong'. Just listen to the statement that there is no actual relationship when two people are living in a conceptual world. If you listen to that, then what does that do to you?

Q: It does nothing to me, until I think of it.

K: No! (Laughs) That is just it. The moment you think of it, then you either compare, say, 'Yes, I have heard that before', or say, 'Yes, let's talk about it, let's find out if you are accurate', and so on. By that time I am gone.

Q: But if I listen to it and neither accept nor decline it, just listen to it...

K: Listen to it. What does it do to you? When I say that people living in a conceptual world destroy every form of human relationship, will you listen to that?

Sir, this is the way I function, I will show it to you. Somebody makes a statement of that kind. I do not think, I do not argue, I let it soak into me. And I see the actuality of it, not a conceptual actuality. I say, 'By Jove, how true that is!'

Q: By that you accept it as fact.

K: No! You see, you are off. (Laughs)

Q: What you are telling me is that it is a fact. What I am saying to you is that in order for me to see that it is a fact, I would have to accept it as a fact.

K: Madam, will you listen to something? Listen, not argue, not say yes, right, wrong. When you are interested, when you are really concerned with total humanity, you are concerned with the individual. But if you are concerned with the individual, then you are not concerned with the total humanity. I wonder if you see what I mean.

Go to India and you see the tremendous riches on one side; and the misery, starvation, poverty, hunger, brutality, everything else that is going on. You go to Europe, you see the suffering, the same thing, chicanery, double-talk, and riches, everything in terms of property, money. And you come here, it is the same thing. So you see the whole of humanity, the whole of it: pleasure, suffering, starvation, pride, arrogance, violence. So you are concerned with the whole of it. What happens when you are concerned with the whole? Then every little thing matters.

So, what shall I do when you are living on one floor and I am living on another? Where shall we meet? That is why I say please listen. First learn the art of listening, then the art of seeing, then, ultimately, the art of learning. So can I listen to you—listen, not compare, not judge, not say, 'Well, what you are saying you have already said, what you are saying a million people have said'—but actually listen? Can you do it? Even when you listen to a bird, you say, 'Well, that is a robin'.

Can you help the student to listen? Do you want to know what I would do? The first thing I would do with a group of students is say, 'Forget lessons, everything, put it all aside. Let us find out what it means to listen'. Listen when I say that I love you, not just to the words but to the feeling that I love you. They would listen, wouldn't they? Because there is some reality there. But if I say, 'Well, I must love you, because this is a concept, that all human beings are brothers, and all live in Jesus, all live in God', or something or other... The first thing I would do in a class is say, 'We are going to see what it means to listen'; first verbally then non-verbally. Can you do it, sir? If you do not listen, can you teach them how to listen?

Can you help the student to listen if you yourself are not listening? If I do not know what it means to listen, how can I tell a student to listen? So I must find out what it means to listen; learn about it. To listen to an aeroplane and not say, 'That is a jet'. Just listen. Listen to a bird and not say, 'Well, that is a nightingale or a blackbird', but just listen. Listen to my wife and not say, 'Well, I know her, it is the old business going over and over again'. Just listen. That would be my first concern with the student. Listening means attention. So you have given him the seed of attention.

Q: Can we cultivate this attention?

K: No, no, that is a concept. You are off. Please, sir, do listen to what I am saying. I said I would help him to learn the art of listening. The art of listening means attention. In that attention there is no movement of thought. That is all. I would say, 'Learn that'. I am going to spend days on that.

Q: Can the child cultivate that attention in him? Can he know when he is not paying attention?

K: No, no, I said do not cultivate. Cultivate means time. Cultivate means I am doing this, cultivating it, growing it, multiplying it. Attention is not multiplication. First I would help him to listen. He can only listen when he is really paying attention. But he has been trained not to pay attention; he is all over the place, he is not listening to anything consistently. So I would do that. So I have planted in him—not I—the seed of attention is planted. The seed does not grow. This is not the seed that grows. It is attention. So I say, 'Now, for the next week or ten days, month, that is the only thing that matters'.

Then the act of listening, which is a pure act of listening. He does not know what it means because he has never been told about it. So I am telling him for the first time. And his attention is wandering. So I have to have patience. This is the most fundamental thing he must learn. On a walk I say, 'Listen to that bird. Do not name it'. I would play with it. I would say, 'Your mind is wandering; go after that, look at that, listen to that, not to the bird'. So he learns the art of listening—not to what I am saying, or somebody else is saying, but the art, the act. Then I would teach him, help him in the art of seeing; seeing things as they are.

Q: Ultimately he would be able to understand his conditioning through this. So we are helping the child to develop, and at points of the child's development he is going to see parts of his conditioning?

K: You see, you bring in the word develop.

Q: Okay, well, that was…

K: No, no, it is very important. I listened to that word! What are you developing in the child?

Q: We are helping the child.

K: No. You are giving him a good body, a healthy body, not to be sick; therefore, right food, right exercise. Inwardly, you are not developing anything. Culture has imposed something on him. By removing the impositions, there is intelligence.

So, the art of listening. And the art of seeing. The art of listening implies great attention and sensitivity. Therefore he will not hurt. Then I would go into the art of learning, and so on, and so on.

Q: If the educator really were without conditioning...

K: No, I did not say that. I said the educator is conditioned, so is the student conditioned. We said both are conditioned. When the educator sees his actual conditioning, he has moved. Then the problem arises of how to deal with the student. Then I say, help him to listen.

Q: But you have a school; you have, now, in actuality, a school with students, with educators.

K: Who are conditioned.

Q: Right. Who have not come to that point.

K: No. I am saying to a teacher in the school: are you listening to the fact or a concept? Are you functioning from the field of concepts or from the field of reality, of actuality?

Q: Right. And his answer is: from the field of concepts.

K: So, move, go into it, find out, work.

Q: But in the meantime...

K: Ah, no meantime. There is no meantime. If he is

working, there is no meantime. It is only when you are not working that the meantime comes in.

CHAPTER 6.

IS IT POSSIBLE TO HAVE INTELLIGENCE WITHOUT EXPERIENCE?

Krishnamurti (K): We have the problem of how to educate our children, the students, who are already conditioned. The teachers are also conditioned. How can they help each other to uncondition themselves? The conditioning is the centuries of weight of tradition, inherited, acquired or passed on from mouth to mouth, or from newspaper to newspaper, so our minds are heavily burdened. And apparently what we are doing, educationally, politically, and religiously, is going round and round in circles, never resolving any problem. When we are confronted with such a state of affairs—politics divorced from ethics, religion divorced from real religiousness, and so on—our response is according to our conditioning. We go around in a peculiar circle thinking that is progress, advancement. So, what is one to do? Can we discuss this, have a dialogue about it?

This has also been a problem in the Indian schools, to transform a student to have a different quality of mind, not a mind that memorizes and gets a job and settles down in life, but a mind that does much more. It cannot do much more if it remains caught in the structure of memory. If you had a son or daughter, what would you do with her or him? Being responsible for the child, how would you help them?

Q: Open the child to experience, to new things, to things that would perhaps help him.

K: Sir, would you question any kind of experience?

Q: What do you mean?

K: Why should I go through any experience? If you say they must go through experiences, which apparently is what you are suggesting, then I must drink, commit murder, do all kinds of things because I must experience life.

Q: No, of course not.

K: No. When you use the word experience, that is what is involved in it.

Q: You cannot in any way expect to be able to say, 'Absolutely you cannot experience this', and feel that your word will be held, because in that case they will not listen. But there are points to which they will listen, if your explanation has the intelligence and the knowledge, upon which they will place faith.

K: I would like to attack this problem differently if I may. We think experiences are necessary—right?—sexual experience, a dozen experiences. I am talking about experiences, not good or bad experiences. We think experiences are necessary for the cultivation of the mind, for the growth of a child, for the understanding of life. Would you agree?

Q: It has been shown to be necessary.

K: I question it. Why should I go through any experience? Please discuss it. Go into it a little bit. If you cultivate intelligence—whatever that word may mean, which we will discuss—why should an intelligent child go through any experience? Does intelligence come into being through experience?

Q: If the mind is deprived of experience, it deteriorates.

K: Which means that without experience you would not be intelligent?

Q: The mind would be distorted and less developed.

K: Ah, I question that very thing. Can the mind be distorted by experience, or does the mind distort experience?

Q: Well, maybe we are disagreeing over what the word experience means.

K: We will go into it, sir. Do think about it a little bit before you attack me. The word experience means to go through. If I experience something, it means I retain what I have experienced as a memory.

Q: So you are speaking of an experience as having a beginning and an end.

K: No sir. The word experience means to go through, go

beyond, to go from where you are, through something, and out. But to us, experience means to go through and collect what you have gone through and retain it as a memory. I experience sex. I experience anger. I experience having plenty of money, or no money, or whatever I experience.

Q: I also experience hammering a nail.

K: Yes. Use all those incidents. Which means that through various experiences you gather memories of each experience. And that collection of memories is what we call an educated mind. That is a mind that says, 'I have been through sex', 'I have been through LSD', 'I have been through peyote', 'I have been through Krishnamurti', 'I have been through Jesus'. I have been through this and that.

Q: 'I have been through reading history'.

K: Yes, history, all that. Which is to gather, accumulate memory, but not to go through to finish and move, but always to collect, gather, acquire. Acquire Transcendental Meditation or another meditation. All of these basically imply collecting knowledge, which is memory, about all these things.

Q: But is there anything else but experience?

K: You say that experience is necessary, and I am questioning whether experience will give intelligence. That is what we say. That is the accepted tradition: 'I have experienced, my boy, so do not go through that. I will give you all the reasons, but do not go through that. I know what it means'. I explain it politely, nicely, affectionately. You might accept it. But you are going to experience something else that I approve of. So we are collecting experiences, acquiring various kinds of knowledge, which is stored up as memory in the brain. Now, is that conducive to intelligence?

If I had a student, would I tell him, 'Go through every experience. Only do not murder, that is dangerous! It does not matter if you take marijuana, that does not do harm. A little alcohol is all right', and so on? Would we encourage him to have experiences?

Q: But what about the things that happen in life, that life itself produces without our seeking them?

K: That is, 'If you go through life, it teaches you'. What? What does life teach me?

Q: Well, that some things can be good and some can be bad.

K: Ah, no. What does life teach me, teach you? Does it teach you anything? We are all so damned traditional.

Q: It may not teach, but things happen. Things happen by our being alive.

K: Please, that is a different matter. I am asking you as a teacher, as a parent, why you would encourage your son or a student to have experience. And you say he must have it because that is conducive to intelligence.

Q: It is conducive to determining many, many things in life. I mentioned hammering a nail for an explicit purpose. If I have to hammer a nail, I do seek experience;

and the more I hammer various nails, the better I hammer a nail. I learn this. This stays with me, this is something that is retained in my memory.

K: That is fairly obvious. You are saying, hammering a nail, riding a bicycle, driving a car, learning a technique, are necessary. That is obvious. You could not come here without driving a car; therefore you had to learn the technique of driving and so on. That is obvious. But does the acquisition of various forms of technique make for intelligence?

What do we mean by intelligence? Not what you or I think intelligence means, offering various opinions that are endless. According to the dictionary, which gives the common usage of the word, intelligence is derived from Greek, Latin, Sanskrit and so on, and means not only to read inter legere, between the lines, but also to have an insight into what you read. Which means having freedom to look, not just accept what you read. That is the meaning of that word. So if you say, 'No, sorry, I do not accept that', then we are off. We must accept the common usage of the word. Lire in French, legere in Italian and so on, means not only to read between the lines but to have an insight into what you read between the lines, and to have an insight into the whole movement of life, not just parts of it. If you accept that meaning of the word, then does experience give that insight?

Q: What do you mean by insight?

K: Ah, no. You are all saying, it means this 'to me'.

Q: Okay, what does it mean?

K: You must find out. Not what it means to me. It means to have sight inside to something. Insight. So we get away from personal opinions which are so deadly in a discussion. To have an insight into politics: to see that when politics is divorced from ethics, then corruption sets in. To have an insight into that is to have clear sight into that problem.

Q: Where does that insight come from?

K: Ah, wait. We are first examining the word insight. We said that when politics is divorced from ethics, there is corruption. Now, to see that as a fact is to have an insight. You know what is happening in the world: politicians have divorced ethics from politics, and therefore there is corruption. Intelligence means that, according to the dictionary, not my opinion or your opinion. So I say to myself: why should I have experience to have an insight?

Q: May I comment on that?

K: No, no, do not comment, sir. I am asking a question. I want to find out. Question, sir, do not accept me as an authority. I am questioning myself. I asked why I should accept tradition which says experience is necessary to have intelligence, that experience equals intelligence. I say to myself, that is the accepted norm, accepted tradition. I reject that. Why should I accept it? I might find a different way of living. So I say: 'Why should I have experience? Why can't I see that to kill somebody is wrong, is a sin', or whatever word you like to use, 'so violence is unnecessary?' Must I go through violence to see that violence does not pay?

Q: It is a marvellous point, Krishnaji, except for one thing. One does not have to experience violence to know violence is evil, but one does know violence is evil through experience, through viewing the evil of others, the violence of others killing. One knows that taking a life is wrong, through experience. Experience must not be experienced merely in the narrow confines of one experience.

K: If you see it is wrong because you have collected various experiences, then why do you allow your sons to be killed in a war?

Q: I would not.

K: Ah, not you, sir, not you! The world. Because you are the result of the world.

Q: Because the world has an insight or an intelligence into their experience different from mine. Their interpretation is what the problem is.

K: Forgive me, but you have not answered my question. I am asking you why experience is necessary to have intelligence.

Q: But I have explained: my experience collectively has given me the insight I now have. You mentioned earlier that politics, when it divests itself of ethics, creates corruption. Having seen this is experience.

K: That is what I am questioning. Please listen. Because I read newspapers, and have seen evidence of politicians all over the world who are not acting ethically, morally, I conclude that when politics is divorced from ethics there is corruption. Do I see it, or is it a conclusion? Go slowly, sir, go slowly.

This is really a very deep and subtle point; which is that conclusions are the result of accumulated experiences. A man who does not act on conclusions, who has no conclusions, sees that politics divorced from ethics brings corruption. It is a fact, not a conclusion. Whereas, if I say that Nixon, Eisenhower, Roosevelt, Kennedy, or Mrs Gandhi, and X, Y, Z have all acted immorally in the political world, and therefore there is corruption, that is a conclusion. I have concluded from observing certain facts, and that is an idea I hold to. Whereas the other man says, 'Observe the fact, do not draw a conclusion, and then you have an insight'.

I want to bring my son up, so I say, 'Please, do not experience anything. Do not ask for experience'. That requires tremendous understanding. It is something new, so he says, 'My God, what are you talking about?' Everybody around me says to have sex at the age of 15, or 13; to experience this, experience that; and here somebody comes saying, 'Do not experience a thing. Try to find out why you should not experience'.

Q: How could a person have insight about politics and ethics if one had not had contact with politics or with ethics?

K: Sir, I have met prime ministers, cabinet ministers, politicians. It is not from that and their crookedness that I have said that politics divorced from ethics is corruption. It is not because I have met all these people. It is so. That is the truth.

Q: Is it from some absolutes?

K: No, it is not from an absolute. It is like gravity; it is so.

Q: You have to experience gravity.

K: Do you mean drop a potato or an apple? You have seen it drop. You do not have to experience gravity.

Q: You experience it every day. The weight of your body is gravity in action. The very fact that you have to lift your leg in order to move forward is an experience.

K: You see, sir, you are not trying to find out what the other fellow is saying. I know all your opinions. You have stated them. Thousands have stated the fact that you must have experience, that otherwise there is no insight, that otherwise there is no intelligence. Millions have said this. That is the tradition. And somebody comes along and says, 'I am sorry, I do not accept that; it all sounds too damn silly'. And you say, 'No, I will prove it to you', and you fight. So we say, please do not fight me, just listen, find out. I know your opinions, I know what you think. I have battled with this problem from the age of 15. Sorry.

Q: But you see, what we are saying is that we feel this. Now, we would like to know how one could determine anything without experience.

K: Please, sir, you never asked. You have always said, 'This is so'. You do not say to me, 'Now, please, let's talk about it, let's find out what you mean by it. You must be crazy, when a hundred million people say that and you come along and say quite the contrary. You must be a nut, a crazy man'. So I say: please, listen to what I have to say, and listen to find out, not to resist, not to say, 'You are wrong'.

I would teach my son or the student, by saying, 'Please listen. A million people accept this. I am saying something totally different, so find out'.

Q: Krishnamurti, I do not think it is a question of resisting you. It is setting up our beliefs about it in such a way that maybe we can look at them. When I point out my thoughts or something, I am not resisting you.

K: Sir, what you have is what a million people have. And along comes somebody who says: 'Please, look at this. Look at it, watch it, examine it. Do not say bang, bang, bang against it, just watch it'.

Q: But he also asks us questions that we answer.

K: Of course, sir, I am doing that. So let us both find out whether it is possible to have intelligence without experience. It is a tremendous problem. If you say, 'I must have experience', then I must get drunk to know what sobriety is. I must have sex in order to understand what celibacy means. I must murder in order to find out what it means to kill, and to see the punishment, and so on. I know all those methods. I know all that you have said, a dozen, million times, in different ways. So I say to you: find out whether it is possible to live without experience and what it means. It means you are constantly experiencing, consciously as well as unconsciously. You say something to me and I react, which is an experience. There is a challenge and a response. That is life, that is constantly taking place, and it is what we call experience.

Challenge, response, adequately or inadequately, and from that inadequacy or adequacy there is a memory which I call experience, and I retain it. This goes on all through life, all the time. Whether I like it or not, it is happening.

Why do you retain what happens in your mind? That is a challenge, and I respond, and the response teaches me something; and that I have learnt; and I hold it in my memory. Isn't that so?

Q: When you say retain, do you mean to dwell on it?

K: Record. The function of the brain is to record.

Q: I understand that. The physical function of the brain is just to record whatever comes in.

K: That is all.

Q: But when you say retain, though, are you saying to dwell on what comes in?

K: No. Retain, store. Not dwell on it. Sir, look. You call me a fool. That is a challenge. I respond either adequately or inadequately. If I respond adequately, there is no recording. It is only when I do not respond adequately that there is recording.

Q: Shouldn't we question what adequate means?

K: I will go into it. Golly! You do not listen to find out. Please, just listen to me. We said all life is challenge and response. That is so, whether that challenge is conscious and the response is conscious, or unconscious, not aware.

This challenge and response is experience. So I say to myself: that is perfectly right, that is what is happening. Experience means to go through and finish, not retain; except technologically.

Q: Why is retaining antithetical to going through?

K: It is only when I do not go through and finish that I hold it. Look, sir, if I hate you because you have done something—challenge and response—this hate goes on, building up. Now, if I understand hate and finish it at the moment of challenge and response, there is no retaining of it, is there? It is finished. I do not hate you; it is gone. I wonder why you do not see this simple fact.

Q: But sir, the experience is still retained. It has happened. I understand what you have showed, but I am adding something to it.

K: No, forgive me, you have not understood what I have said.

Q: But very certainly I have. Your emotion has ceased to continue; you have ceased to continue with hatred. But, unless you have a completely blank memory, the action, having occurred, will be stored somewhere in your mind.

K: No. If you go into it deeply, you will see it is not necessary to hold anything in the mind, except technological things. You have not gone into it.

Look sir, we said challenge and response is the process of experiencing. We all agree to that, don't we? That is fairly simple. Not simple—I am not clever, please. Why should my mind be burdened with all these things? You hate me, or somebody likes me; somebody says, 'Oh, marvellous', this or that; why should I hold it all in my brain? What is the point of it? So, you ask a much more important question, which is: are we acting mechanically, or can the mind be free of all these burdens?

Q: If the brain is an instrument for recording, which it is as I understand it, then I do not understand how you let go.

K: I will show it to you. First see the fact. Part of our brain is a recording machine. We have given to that part tremendous importance, and neglected the other part. Our education, our relationship, everything is in the field of memory. That is obvious, sir. So, I am asking: is the mind mechanical? If we only act in that part of the brain which is the area of memory, it is mechanical. Which is what we are doing. It is a tradition, like saying that everybody must have experience. That is part of memory. So I am asking: is our mind mechanical? And it is, obviously. I read algebra and so on, and memorize. I function in the factory, in business—it is all memory. And in my relationship with my wife, it is still memory. So, my life has become mechanical.

Q: Well, one need not automatically respond to a challenge.

K: No, you may turn away from it. But I am asking something else. You are going back. Forgive me, please. I am asking: is your mind, our mind—your mind is my mind, we are the world—is our mind mechanical? Is our life mechanical? Job, factory, you know, the whole thing. So experience, according to you, has led me, my son, or another, into a mechanical field. And that is what we call education. And from that area we act; skilfully, adequately or inadequately, brutishly. So, look what has happened. People who have insisted that experience is necessary for intelligence have reduced life to a mechanical process. Their religions are mechanical. They believe in God or do not believe in God. I am just a mechanical entity with occasional flair for freedom, hoping for freedom. So experience has made me a stupid, mechanical, cunning, shameless entity; I can repeat all that everybody has said.

My next question is: why have people given such enormous importance to experience? Why has humanity given such importance to experience as knowledge? Come on, this is what you are training your children for!

Q: Because we do not know how to live without experience.

K: Ah! No. You will find out. Push. Why have human beings given such importance to this? Perhaps because they say this will give them security, that knowledge is security.

Q: And importance. Knowledge, this kind of knowledge gives one security and a sense of importance.

K: Yes, you have given tremendous importance to it. Why?

Q: Because that is what people want.

K: They want drugs, they want sex, they want vulgarity, they want all the bestialities of the world. But we are asking why human beings have made knowledge a most colossally important thing, why all the volumes say there is security in knowledge. Knowledge has given me security. It gives me a job. I know my wife. I am certain of her. That is security.

Q: But I will hang on to a false belief, even though I realize it is a false belief, because it is security.

K: I said knowledge has become important because we think it will give us physical, psychological, spiritual security. This is a fact. If I am a Catholic, I am completely secure in a Catholic world. The beliefs may be the most superstitious nonsense, but they give me security. If I am in Russia, in Moscow, it gives me tremendous security to say, 'Yes'. So knowledge, apparently, has given us security. It certainly has given us security in the world of technique: I can drive a car, and so on. But has knowledge given us security in any other field?

Q: Sir, even in the field of technique it does not give complete security because when you drive a car something might happen.

K: Of course, but has psychological knowledge of myself given me security? There have been a thousand books about myself—which is yourself. People go to Africa to study animals in order to give me security. Has it given me security?

Q: We can see that it has not given us security, but that makes us think that we do not have the right kind of knowledge or enough knowledge.

K: Ah, that is another crooked way of thinking: 'Give us more knowledge'.

Q: Why do we ask for security?

K: Where is security? Which you must have, otherwise the brain can not function properly.

Q: Well, it is physical.

K: No, go into it, sir, a little more. The brain needs security, which means food, clothes, shelter. Otherwise you cannot function. And psychologically it must have security.

Q: I do not know. I am not sure.

K: Wait, wait. Psychologically it must be clear. So, people say, 'Study your behaviour, learn about yourself; that will give security'. All the Freudians, Jungians, and the analysts say, 'Learn, find out, analyse so that you have more knowledge. That knowledge will give you security'. But is there security psychologically? Is there security in my knowing my psyche? Which is knowledge. As there is security in the physical world of technology. I say I must have the same kind of security inwardly, so I read Freud, I read Jung, this and that. And I ask what you mean by security. Are you secure with your wife?

Is there security? Go slowly, sir, you will see something for yourself. Once you understand this, the thing is simple. Is there security? The brain must have complete security, otherwise it seeks security in neuroticism, in beliefs, in experiences, in conclusions, in fantasies, in mysticism, and so on. So it must have security. It has found security in the technological world. Even there, there is no security because there are wars—which are built up psychologically. I wonder if you see it.

Psychologically I want pleasure, I want to go somewhere, I want to enjoy myself, I must fulfil my desires, I must go to Los Angeles today because there is a new film on, or something or other. The brain needs complete security. I see it is necessary in the physical world—food, clothes, and shelter. I must have that, human beings must have that. But why don't they have that? Because they are seeking security in the world which is unreal. When I say, 'I am a Hindu', and, 'My country is better than your country', that is a psychological fantasy, unreal. That unreality divides people. So there is no physical security. This is so simple. If there were no "American", no "Englishman", no "Indian", no "Muslim", no this or that, no patriotism, no waving flags—what?

So, now to see. We see that in the technological world there must be security, and we want security psychologically. To say, 'I am an American', gives a tremendous sense of security: two hundred million people, prosperous, enjoying cars and all the rest of it, and I am one of them. But that psychological unreality in which I have sought security destroys physical security by dividing nations. So I say: 'By Jove, look, there is security only in seeing the false as the false. It is false to say I am an Indian, or an American, or Muslim, or Catholic. It is a non-reality'.

Q: So one could say that the feeling of insecurity that one has is a symptom of the false world that one lives in.

K: Of course. To have an insight into that is to see that there is psychological division, which is "my" India and "your" America. The psychological difference is destroying the world. To see that psychological division is destroying the world is an insight. See that; then you are free of nationalities. So, there is security—not in experience, not in knowledge—but only in intelligence. Which is to have an insight into everything. I have an insight that all organized religions are nonsense, propaganda. Finished; I do not belong to any religion. Therefore I can find out if there is or there is not God. I can inquire.

I want to teach my son to live without experience. I wonder if you understand what it means. He will have sex. He will have to have various so-called challenges and responses, physically, emotionally and intellectually. That is life, flowing in and out all the time. But the moment he is not flowing but retaining, then he becomes mechanical. Then he says, as a million people say, 'Experience is absolutely necessary'. They are dead people, generally.

Q: If you put a small child on the ground and put a rattlesnake next to the child, the child hears the rattle, walks over, picks up the snake—bang, no more small child. If the child sees a rattlesnake striking at it behind glass, and is frightened by it: experience, realization, knowledge of danger, insight. It has determined or it has an insight, and it will not again play with a rattlesnake. But it must experience it to know that.

K: Yes sir, you are going back to your old theory, maintaining at any price your assertion that knowledge through experience is necessary. Finished. All right, there is nothing more to be said.

Q: No, no, there is more to be said, because what I am saying is that I have listened to everything you have said and have grasped everything you said. Of course, the insight you pointed out was very true. But the insight I am pointing out is not true. Do you follow what I say?

K: Oh yes, I follow. Sir, please forgive me. When I go to India and talk about different things, they say, 'You are crazy. To live without experience, what are you talking about?' I put it differently and use different sets of words, but it comes to the same thing. Sir, to put it all very simply, we have worshipped knowledge. Bronowski in The Ascent of Man on television, has been saying knowledge, knowledge, knowledge; the democracy of knowledge, the integrity of knowledge, and the growth of mankind through knowledge. That is the accepted norm, the accepted tradition, by the scientists, by the Pope, by the gurus. Everybody says this. Everybody. And a poor chap comes along and says, 'Look, there may be a different way of living'. And you say, 'Get thee behind me, Satana'. That is all. You do not say, 'Now, what are you talking about? Let's find out'.

We can discuss this, sir. Can you live—daily, not theoretically—without seeking psychological security in your wife, in your work, in your thinking, in your behaviour?

I would talk to the child. I would say, 'Some people say to have experience at any price. Acquire knowledge through experience, not only in the technological world but also in the psychological world, in the so-called spiritual world, in the whole structure. That is what the world—you, your parents, your society, your friends—say'. That is the fact; that is what they are saying. 'Examine this', I would say, 'there is something totally different from that. Now let's talk about it'. I would go into it with him; how people have worshipped things made by the hand or by the mind—a statue, a cross, a symbol—because that gives tremendous security, for the whole Christian world, for the whole Hindu world. The Muslim world does not have statues but they have scriptures. I would point all this out to him. 'Do not choose. Have an insight. Find out what it means to have an insight. See what is involved. When you drive a car, learn a language, it is mechanical. Insight demands a totally different kind of mind, which is non-mechanistic'.

I would talk for days about this, go into it. If he chooses, he is lost, because he is choosing out of confusion. He does not know, poor chap. He says, 'I like you, sir, so I will choose this'. And when he marries, he says, 'Yes darling, all right, let's go back to something else'.

Q: Here we are going to have a school with ages from 4 or 5 and on through. With 4, 5, 6 year-olds we cannot have extensive talks.

K: You cannot. Sir, they do not understand all this. You cannot explain all this to 5 or 6 year-olds. You can help them even then, but not by arguments, by words, or by example. That is dreadful. I would approach it differently. I would say, 'Why do you accept tradition?'

Q: But asking a question like that of a 12 year-old…

K: No, I do not. I am asking you. I would put the question differently to a 12 year-old: 'Why do you follow people? Why do you belong to this group, that group, the other?' I would put it differently. That is irrelevant. I would say,

'Why does humanity accept authority? The word authority derives from the word author, one who originates; one has originated something; then others accept it and make it into an authority. So why do you follow anybody? Why do you accept tradition?'

And then you would say, 'Sir, there is good tradition, bad tradition'. (Laughs)

Q: Here, though, I sense a number of people who do not follow authority.

K: Sir, the whole world follows. The whole world is based on following, accepting and obeying.

Q: No, I believe that we, this group, follow through experience.

K: Ah! (Laughter) We are back to the good old stuff.

Q: You asked, 'What is the difference?' There is a great difference, a vast difference.

K: Sir, Transcendental Meditation people are following because they want an experience of peace.

Q: No! On the contrary. Following that is not experience as we are talking of it. What they are doing is accepting rather than challenging through their own experience.

K: (Laughs) No, on the contrary, they say, 'We have experienced this astonishing peace. This is our experience. You call it stupid, but we have experienced it'.

Q: I do not call it that. I have an insight into it.

K: Ah, no! They say—if you use the word experience—'We have experienced this astonishing peace in us. By getting the mantra, by paying 150 dollars', whatever it is, 'we have got it'. And you say, 'How ridiculous that is!' But you insist on experience. My experience is as good as yours.

Q: Yes, but when I see the ridiculousness of it through experience, I gain an insight.

K: You cannot gain insight through experience. That is what I have been saying.

Q: Many of the things you have said have not expressed this to me. Reading history, reading a book is an experience; looking at a thing is also an experience. You do not have to kill to understand death if you can gain it from reading a story about death. That is an experience also.

Q: But he spoke of experience as a piece of knowledge that you retain. That is how he defined experience.

Q: But the question is: why experience at all?

K: We reduce this to absurdity.

Q: May I ask you something? People whom we call authorities are the authors of this false world that we live in. Is that correct?

K: Why do you call it a false world?

Q: Well, we spoke of the false world as being the world that gives us insecurity.

K: Sir, no. It is a very alive, dreadful world we live in. It is not a false world. People throw bombs. That is not a false world.

Q: But there are ideas behind the throwing of the bombs.

K: That is it.

Q: But these authorities are the authors of beliefs and the ideas of the psychological world in which we live. Why then do we feel the necessity to live in these false beliefs? We went into that a little bit last time.

K: Because it means security.

Q: But they in themselves give us insecurity.

K: Yes sir, but that comes later.

Q: In other words, if we did not have these false beliefs and so forth…

K: Not false, sir, do not use the word false.

Q: Okay. If we did not have these beliefs and these ideas, then why would we feel psychologically insecure?

K: But you do have them. Sir, look. I do not know if you have heard of the ancient Hindu scripture, the Rig Veda. In that, there is no mention of God at all. You understand, sir? In that book, in that literature called the Rig Veda, there is no mention of God. But later some said, 'That is much too simple, let's complicate it'. From that came the various other Vedas within which they mention God, priests, rituals. Man invented all this to get profit out of it.

So, can I teach my son, my daughter, my student to understand the full significance of experience? The significance, the meaning, the inwardness of it; not, must have experience or not have experience, but for him or her to understand the meaning of that word and what is implied in it, what man has done with it. Expose all that to them. Can I do that? At the age of 5 or 12? As they become older, it becomes more difficult because they say, 'Sorry, I haven't time for all that because I have to pass an exam'. Or, 'Why do you bring this new stuff in, I am not interested'. So can I, as an educator, help them to understand the meaning of that word? Can you help them—not say 'deny experience' or 'accept experience'—to see the implications of all this? I think you can if you, yourself, see the implications.

Q: The teachers here who see the implications are going to be able to work with the youngsters and help them. But surely we are going to be confronted in the school with educators who do not.

K: Therefore the educator has to be educated.

Q: All right. In the process, while I am helping the educator, supposedly…

K: I am educating myself.

Q: He is still going to be dealing with children while we are helping him, so to speak. Can he then help that child he is working with while he is still very much learning himself?

K: Of course. Sir, suppose you know how to play tennis.

By teaching me how to play tennis, you learn more, don't you? Yes.

CHAPTER 7.

THE PURE ACT OF LEARNING

Krishnamurti (K): We have been considering what is happening in the world, the violence, the tremendous class prejudices, colour prejudice, wars, and the lack of real relationship between human beings; the national divisions, economic divisions, all the religious dogmatism with its separative activities. We have been talking about this and asking what kind of education a human being must have in order to meet this crisis, this state of the world. What is the correct education students should have so that they can adequately, sanely meet this?

What do you think is the cause of all this? I know there are multiple reasons, various activities which are bringing about great pressures on people. What do you think is the basic cause or the root of all this human mess?

Questioner (Q): I think that it is just general lack of concern for fellow human beings, and lack of emphasis on our relationships.

K: I wonder. Is that it? Is it as simple as that, just lack of affection, lack of care, lack of love, lack of compassion?

Do you think that is the only thing? That may be the real thing. Let's put it round the other way. If you had children, what kind of education would you want them to have?

Q: Well, certainly not one that just emphasizes their intellectual development. I would want more for them than that.

K: What do you mean by the word intellect? Intellect also implies intelligence, also implies capacity to think clearly, reasonably, sanely, impersonally. That is the essence of intellectual capacity, to observe and to act totally objectively, impersonally. That is the meaning that is implied when you say, 'He is a very intellectual man', he only looks at facts, and observes activities, and calculates. Is that what you mean by the intellect?

Q: Yes, essentially.

K: The universities throughout the world are filled with people who have the capacity to store up a great deal of knowledge in their brains and act skilfully with that knowledge. That is generally what is happening throughout the world: get a degree in the technological world or in the humanities or in the arts and so on; get degrees, get a job, marry, and settle down. That is what is happening. Is that what you want for your sons, your daughters, your friends?

Q: No.

K: Then why are we being educated?

Q: I think in many cases we are being educated because

there are people who would educate us in order to manipulate us.

K: In the totalitarian world, that obviously is so, isn't it?

Q: Well, I think there is a bit of that.

K: Sir, when politics is divorced from ethics, or business is divorced from ethics, or professors are divorced from ethics, you must have corruption, and that is going on right throughout the world. What kind of education must we have to face all this?

Q: I think we need an education that would teach children to cope with all the problems and anxieties of the world without becoming totally enmeshed in them.

K: How would you do it? That means what?

Q: Well, that means bringing a child totally to understand himself and his nature.

K: Go slowly, sir, a little bit slowly. Understanding: who will help him? The educator?

Q: Well, it depends on the educator's point of view.

K: On the educator, essentially, and the parents. It is not just on the educator alone, the parents are equally responsible. So it is a triangular process: the parent, the child, and the educator.

Q: Right.

K: Now, what does society demand? What do the politicians with their manipulations want? What does the technological world want? There are all these pressures on the young child as well as on the teacher and on the parents. This process is going on. If we are interested in education, as a parent, as an educator, what shall we do? What is the process of unravelling for the parent, the educator, and the child? Because they are all caught in this.

Q: Well, the first thing is to remove them from being enmeshed in the whole of that system.

K: Yes, but how? The parents must be interested in this.

Q: If the parents are operating within the structure of society, and they are dissatisfied with it, they must be aware of what it is in society that dissatisfies them.

K: Is it a matter of being satisfied? Some may be satisfied. Is that the criterion?

Q: Well, there are degrees of that. If someone is satisfied with mediocrity, then they would reach a certain level and just stay there without trying to improve themselves, without trying to find out how to live with other people in a more creative way.

K: Sir, forgive me, you are using words like creative. Words have specific dictionary meanings; therefore we must be a little bit careful in the usage of words, because words have power, words have significance by themselves, not just according to what you or I give to them. Suppose I am dissatisfied with society as it is. Personally, I think society as it is, is totally immoral. I am not dissatisfied, I see it is immoral.

Q: All right, you are not dissatisfied, but you are dissatisfied with society.

K: No, that is the difference. I see that society is immoral. It is not that I am dissatisfied. It is a fact. Why should I be dissatisfied with a fact? I see that the structure of society, whether it is in India, in Europe or anywhere else, is immoral, in the sense non-ethical. That is a fact. Why should I be dissatisfied with a fact? It is so. What is important is how I meet the fact. If I am dissatisfied with the fact, then I want another fact which will satisfy me.

Q: Well, then how do we meet the fact?

K: That is the question. So let us move away from satisfaction, from what I want. You can be satisfied by one thing, I will be satisfied by another. But if both of us are concerned with fact, then we can do something.

Society as it is is immoral. That is a fact. How will the educator or the parent educate the student to realize it as a fact, and act? Not act according to the educator or to the parent, then you go back to satisfaction, opinion, judgment. Does the educator, the parent, see the fact that in their own lives—which is the very essence of society—they are immoral?

Q: Unless they discover their own ethics or discover ethics, they will not be able to live ethically.

K: It is not your ethics or my ethics or their ethics. In India, Europe, one sees—not as an opinion or a judgment—that the structure, the nature of the existing society is corrupt, immoral. That is a fact. How shall I educate my son or the student to see the fact and not act according to his personal like and dislike, opinion, judgment which are very small?

Q: I am not sure that I understand. You are saying be aware of the fact that it is immoral and do not make judgments?

K: Look, I say society is immoral. You and I realize it. What is society? Something out there, or in here?

Q: People.

K: It is my relationship with you that creates society. Put in the most simplistic form, my relationship with you, with my friend, with my neighbour, is the structure of society. If I am corrupt, then my relationship is corrupt. So, do I realize the fact that I am corrupt, that I am immoral? Or do I say, 'Society is immoral'? Do I realize that if I, as part of society, am not moral, society is immoral? Is that a concept, a theory, or a fact?

Q: A fact.

K: Let's be clear. It is a fact.

Q: There surely must be some people within the structure of the society who are moral.

K: I do not know. That may be, may not be. That is irrelevant.

Q: But then society is still immoral even if there are people who are moral.

K: Of course, there may be, that is not our concern. Our concern is that we have to educate students, educate our children. How shall the student, when he grows up, meet this immoral society? That is the point we are discussing.

We say, in the most simple form, society is my relationship with another. It becomes very complex later, but in its simplest form it is human relationship. And if I am corrupt, if I am unethical, my relationship with the whole of humanity is unethical. Do I realize I am the source of immorality? It is not out there. Do I realize that, as a parent, I am responsible, and does the educator also see that he is responsible?

Together, how shall we deal with the student, who is already caught in the immoral structure? Because they are young boys or girls, they are already thinking in terms of what society has imposed on them. You are immoral and the educator is immoral, what shall we do?

Q: I think you have to start by trying to undo what society has done.

K: What? I am society, my lady.

Q: Well, change yourself then.

K: Now wait. How do I change myself? What makes human beings change? There are only two things: profit and punishment. That is a fact.

Q: Then there is no hope. If those are the only two things that change us.

K: Wait sir, you will see it presently. Go into it, sir. All our religions say, 'Do this, and you will go to heaven', which is reward. 'If you do not do this, you will be punished'. In education, when you are a boy, you are given marks, you pass examinations. It is all the same process.

Q: Well, we can see from our society now that the way we have been doing it is bringing us punishment.

K: So you want reward?

Q: It would seem that you would have to begin, as an educator or as a parent, by somehow trying to avoid looking at the world in terms of moral and immoral.

K: But think of it, sir. I live in a world which I, as a human being, have created,. We have created this as human beings.

Q: How can you say that you have created it, if it in actuality has created you? It seems to me that you are saying that if I am immoral, since I am society, society is immoral. I would think the reverse is true, because we are products of society.

K: But who created society? Human beings have created it, haven't they, sir?

Q: But society is not an end. It is a means too.

K: Yes sir, but we said society is the basis of human relationship. It is based on that. If my relationship is not right, then the social structure which I create will be not right. That is all. Do I realize that as a parent, do I realize it as an educator? Do I realize the fact that as long as I am corrupt I cannot help the student?

Q: Well, then you are saying every educator would have to be not corrupt.

K: That is right.

Q: That is very optimistic. (Laughs)

K: We have a school here, so let us find out how to deal with this fact. The educator, the parent and the student are caught in this. The student comes already caught in the social structure: messy, corrupt, conditioned. How shall we, the parents, the educator and the student, deal with that?

Q: If we had an educator who was not corrupt, then we could start the process of creating a student who was not corrupt, and therefore a society.

K: So you say, 'We will wait until we find someone perfect'.

Q: Someone who has an interest in this.

K: We are doing that, sir. The educator, the student and the parent have the same problem. What shall we do?

Q: Well, I do not want to wait around for an educator who is not corrupt.

K: No, quite right. So what will you do? Suppose I am the parent and you are the educator and we have a student. What shall we do? You are conditioned, I am conditioned, and he is conditioned. The three of us are in the same boat. What shall we do?

Q: We can listen to one another.

K: We can listen to one another. Are you listening to me? Do you know what it means to listen?

Q: I think so.

K: The gentleman suggested listening. Do I listen to you the educator? Do I listen to the student, and do I listen to myself? Do you understand what I mean? Listen! What do I think, what do I feel, what are my motives, what are my intentions? Do I listen to all the activities that are going on inside me?

Q: You should.

K: Ah, not should! Do you? That gentleman suggested: learn to listen. So, do I listen to anything, or am I always hearing and interpreting according to my pleasure, dislike, prejudice? I am never listening. So I must learn the art of listening.

Q: Right.

K: Will you? Are you listening?

You see, unless one is very serious you cannot go into all this. To me, this is very, serious. Because I am connected with various schools in India, in England, and here, to me this is really an extraordinarily important thing. Not only because I happen to be connected; in itself it is important.

There are these three entities, the parent, the educator, and the child. All of them, because they are human beings, have created a society, in which they live, which is corrupt, immoral. We want to educate each other and the child at the same time, not educate myself first and then pass it on to you. Together, you and I and the child educate ourselves. Is that possible?

Q: Yes.

K: Ah, no! You say yes. Is any parent willing to give up drinking, smoking, being violent, aggressive? You say, 'Please, take my child, look after him, make him intelligent, and I will carry on my life'. So where are the parents, where are the educators who say, 'Look, for the love of my child, I will give up something'? Are there such parents? There are, fortunately for us. Then suppose I am a parent. I say, 'All right, I see drugs are not necessary. Alcohol upsets the brain'. The American custom is to drink a great deal, so I say, 'All right, I will give it up. I won't drink, I won't smoke, I won't take drugs, because it is going to affect my son'. And the educator must do the same. Together we must do it, not I do it and you do not.

If we do that, what takes place? You see that you are conditioned, corrupt, immoral; and so does the parent. Then what takes place between us and the students? We have to teach them mathematics, we have to teach them behaviour, history, geography, and so on. How shall I teach them so that they learn the art of learning? Do we learn or do we merely memorize? Do you see the difference between the two? Which is it we do?

Q: We memorize.

K: We memorize, collect a lot of information, store it in the brain and use it in our daily activities. That is the cultivation of memory to make what we call a very learned person. So is that what we mean by education?

To cultivate one part of the brain, which is structured on memory, knowledge, and keep only that part active? Is that what you want?

Q: No.

K: Do not say no. That is what the whole world wants. All the universities are based on that. Go to Oxford, Cambridge, or the Sorbonne, or come to any of the big universities in this part of the world; they are all concerned with the cultivation of the brain which stores up knowledge or memory. And we call that learning. Is that learning?

One has to find out what learning is. That is also part of learning, isn't it? The cultivation of memory: driving a car is part of memory. So, what is learning? What do you mean by learning?

Q: Taking that which you have put into your mind as facts or memory and being able to use it.

K: That is what we have done, sir. That is what all the universities have trained us to do—skilfully, adequately, or unskilfully, personally, nationally, destructively to make instruments of war. All that is what we have done.

Q: I have memory plus the understanding or the comprehension.

K: We have not come to that yet. I am asking what we mean by learning. Everybody talks about it. And what you all have seen is the accumulation of information as knowledge, and using it as skilfully as possible and as cleverly as possible, as selfishly as possible, as aggressively as possible. That is all.

The word school comes from Greek, and means leisure. A school means a place of leisure. It is only when you have leisure that you can learn. You have leisure here; so you can talk things over and you can investigate and find out. If you had no leisure you could not sit here. You would not. When you have leisure you can learn. So what do we mean by learning?

Q: An experience of discovery?

K: You go to a person to learn. What do you learn? What are you learning now?

Q: I am learning what learning is.

K: Wait. Here we are. What are we learning?

Q: It seems to me we are learning to probe, to investigate.

K: No, please. When we use the word learn, what is implied in that word? You are learning something from the speaker. Are you? Therefore the speaker becomes the authority.

Q: You can learn something from us, perhaps, and that does not give us authority.

K: A professor is an authority.

Q: Only because he is in an office.

K: He is an authority whether he is in the office or at home. He is the authority on something he knows, and he passes on to you what he knows. Is that learning? That is only part of learning, isn't it? You are learning something from somebody, which is, generally, accumulation of information, knowledge. That is a very limited meaning of that word learning.

Q: But many times the professor or the teacher or whatever, instead of imparting knowledge, will stimulate the other party into searching for himself.

K: So you depend on stimulation.

Q: Well, I think there is stimulation.

K: Ah, wait! When you use the word stimulation, it implies every form of stimulation—coffee, tea, drugs, tobacco—every form that stimulates you.

Q: Well, perhaps a better word would be catalyst.

K: No, I would like to stick to this one word, learning, for the time being.

Q: Learning would be like listening or looking or seeing.

K: We are going to find out. We are going to find out.

Q: Well, we are taking such a long time. (Laughter)

K: If I told you in two words, would you learn? Would you? Learning means a non-accumulating process.

Q: Non-accumulating?

K: You see, you have not understood.

Q: No, I haven't.

K: I accumulate information from another, which I call knowledge. To that knowledge, one can add more and more, or take away. That is what we generally call education. That is a very small part of learning. I ask myself what learning is. What is the pure act of learning? I know the other; therefore the act of learning is non-accumulative. Non-accumulative; therefore the mind is free. A mind filled with knowledge is never free, but a mind that is not acquiring experience, knowledge, getting better, becoming more, such a mind is enormous. It is free.

Q: Free to do what?

K: Ah! Why do you say free to do what? Why should it do anything? It is free.

Q: Well, freedom implies the ability to do whatever you want.

K: Is there learning without storing up? Do you understand my question now? I know how to store up. I am used to that. All my tradition, all history, all the educational business is the storing up. I am asking if there is a learning which is never storing anything; and therefore a mind that is free to observe.

Q: But that would mean to be without a motive, totally without a motive.

K: Of course, sir. Follow all that. The motive lies in having knowledge and wanting to use it. Using it you say, 'Will it be profitable or painful?' and so on.

To come back: how am I as an educator or as a parent

to educate the child, the student, so that he learns, not accumulates? This is a problem you probably have never gone into. Sorry to bring it up. So this is a very complex problem, because it implies a mind that is non-mechanistic.

Q: Do you agree that the storing-up process is still a part of learning?

K: A very small part. Of course.

Q: Well, if you learn something even in the sense that you are talking of, and then you do not retain it, I do not see any sense in it.

K: Sir, look, our education consists in storing up.

Q: To a large degree, I would say.

K: What do you mean, to a large degree? Knowledge is what education implies.

Q: Yes, but there are times when I have come across ideas that, no matter how much knowledge I have, I do not know a thing. Whatever I have stored up does not help me, and then I have to think.

K: So, what is thinking? You used the word. What do you mean by thinking?

Q: It is just trying to grasp something.

K: Look at it, sir. I ask you how far it is from here to Santa Barbara. As you know it very well you say, 33 miles or 40 miles, because you are familiar with it. If I ask you a question that is much more complex, there is an interval before you answer it. So what is taking place in the interval, which is time? What is taking place there?

Q: Then I am thinking.

K: Which is what? Go on, sir, slowly, slowly. You will see it in a minute.

Q: I am just looking for the answer.

K: Where are you looking?

Q: Perhaps in that storing-up, perhaps not.

K: Of course! So you are looking into the storage. Looking into the storage, into the memory, is part of thinking.

Q: That is right.

K: So thinking is the response of memory.

Q: I do not know if it is that simple.

K: Sir, look, I asked you, 'What is the distance from here to Santa Barbara?' Quickly there is a response. You do not think, because you are familiar with it, it is stored up. If I ask you a very complex question, you look through books or look into your memory to find the answer.

All that takes time.

Q: Using the experiences that you have had, which is memory.

K: Yes. Memory is the result of experience. Human beings

have had experiences, stored them up, and that memory is called upon, and you give the answer.

Q: You use your memory to apply it to new situations.

K: So memory is the very structure of thought. That is all. Thinking is the response of memory. A surgeon, when he operates, has collected a tremendous amount of information. He uses that information skilfully with his hands.

So, can we educate the child? As a parent, as an educator, knowing that I am corrupt, how am I to uncondition myself, and the student?

Q: The conditioning is memory, right?

K: Obviously. But I must have memory, otherwise I could not walk, I could not drive a car, I could not speak.

Look sir. Just a minute. There are flowers there. Can you look at them? You see them, don't you?

Q: Yes.

K: What happens when you see them? What actually do you do when you see flowers of that kind?

Q: I recall from my memory that that is something called a flower.

K: "Flower": you name it, you see the colour, which is memory, and the word is memory. So what happens? Do you actually see the flower, see that thing, or is memory seeing it? So is there a perception without the word?

Q: If there is, you could not say much more about it than to answer the question yes or no.

K: You must go much deeper than this. You can do that with a flower fairly simply. If you watch your own mind, your own reactions, you know how the words distort the fact. But can you look at your neighbour, your wife, or your husband, without all the structure of memory interfering?

Q: Your memory is always there. You cannot wipe it out.

K: So, you cannot wipe it out. Have you ever tried to look at somebody who has been very close to you—sexually, comfortably, and so on—without having the picture of that person, without looking through the picture, through the image you have built up? Try it. Find out what it means, whether the mind can ever do that. Then you have right relationship with a person, not with an image.

If you are concerned with education, first I would suggest to the parent and to the educator to find out the art of listening; not accepting, not denying, but listening. Listening to your prejudices, listening to your judgment. So you begin to learn how to listen. That is the first thing I would talk about to the student, to the parent, to the educator. I would say, 'Look, let's find out what it means to listen. Can you listen without interpretation? Can you listen without comparison? Can you listen without all your intellectual cunningness; just listen?' That is a great art, isn't it? You listen respectfully to a man whom you think knows, but you do not listen with the same respect to a man who is supposed to be ignorant. So in the art of learning you begin to discover the various degrees and capacities of listening, which show that your own prejudices, your own ambitions, your own motives, your own snobbishness are all involved in the act of listening.

I would talk to the student. I would say, 'Forget everything. Let us find out what it means to listen to the birds, to the wind'. Out there first. Begin objectively and then come closer and closer and closer: 'Can you listen to yourself, your thoughts, your attitudes, your opinions, your like and dislike, the whole of that?'

That means the student, the educator and the parent must have leisure. And the school is the place for leisure. That is why the students go to school. That is what we must provide.

Q: But you can be so busy helping a school to survive that you do not have much leisure to give to the kids.

K: I know. That is one of our difficulties. And when you have built it up, you have no leisure because you have five hundred students. So we must keep it small. We are doing that.

Do you know what it means to see—the art of seeing? We went somewhat into the question of the art of listening. Then there is the art of seeing. Have you ever looked at anything? It is very difficult to see the proportions of the room, the colour of the walls without bringing your prejudices in; just to see the height, the depth of the room, the colours of the books; just to look, not saying you like or do not like. Just to see!

Then, can you see your own thoughts? I would talk to the

students about all that, what it means to see. Not only to see objectively, but what it means to see inwardly. When you see a statue, there is a distance between it and the observer. There is a distance between that object and the observer; the observer who sees through the eyes—vision, light, reflection. There is a distance, isn't there?

Q: There appears to be.

K: No, no, factually, sir.

Q: Physically?

K: Physically.

Q: Yes.

K: To touch it, I must move from here to go there. That is distance. That means time. Now, is there a seeing without distance, without time?

Q: Yes.

K: Do not say yes too quickly. This is really complex, sir. I look at that statue. I know it is the head of the Buddha from sixth century Gandhara. When in India, under Alexander, the Greeks left their architecture, their statues and so on. I see that. The observer is different from the observed.

Q: Physically.

K: The observer is different from that. Obviously. The observer looks at that lamp, and the lamp is not the observer. Right? Now, is there observation in which the observer is the observed? This is really a question of meditation. All kinds of things are involved in this.

It matters enormously how you observe; whether you can observe yourself without the observer. That means there is no division between the observer and the observed. Then that means no conflict.

The Arab and the Jew are fighting, but they are both human beings. It is their conditioning that is making them fight. Hindus and Muslims are fighting in India. It is their conditioning that is dividing them. So division means conflict. When I am divided from my wife, I must have conflict with her.

Human beings have lived in conflict. It is part of their tradition, part of their culture, part of their conditioning to be in conflict—with yourself, with your neighbour, inside yourself. Everything is conflict, and therefore there is violence. So if you would resolve violence and therefore resolve conflict, you have to find out how to live without conflict. Conflict means division. Which is, 'I am this, I will be that'. 'I am this. I am angry today but one day I will not be angry'. That is the division. So there is conflict.

I would help my students to find out how to live without conflict, because to live without conflict is the most marvellous thing on earth. It means no division in oneself, no contradiction in oneself; which implies no ideals at all; because if I have an ideal, there is a division. Therefore there is conflict. So I am this. Can that be transformed? But not to become that.

You see, we have made our life into such an awful mess.

From childhood until we die we have perpetual conflict: wanting, not wanting, being punished, being rewarded, trying to be something, trying not to be something—this perpetual struggle. Out of that comes all our violence. And therefore no love, no affection, no consideration.

So is it possible to live without a single conflict? Which means the observer is the observed. The observer says, 'I am angry'. Then he says, 'I must not be angry'. So he tries to suppress anger, control it, justify it. But if he says, 'I am anger', not, 'I am angry'—if I am that thing which I have named as anger—then a totally different process takes place. You try it sometime. Not try it; do it!

Q: Are you saying that, as a teacher, once you go into the listening and the seeing, then learning comes simultaneously with that, or there is another part to go into?

K: Of course, sir, there is the art of listening, art of learning, art of seeing. They are all one, but nobody has talked about listening and the art of it, the beauty of listening. The word art means to put things in their right place. I hear the politician and I know exactly where to put him. I hear a guru; I know he trots out what he has learnt, his tradition. I listen, and therefore I see clearly how things are out there. I see the world as it is.

Also I see exactly what is going on inside me, my reaction to the world. I am the world. I am not separate from the world. But I have separated myself from the world and said, 'I am an individual'. But I am not. I am part of that. So I am the world. And I watch, and I listen to all the things human beings have done, have created, have quarrelled about. Because I am that. So I am listening to myself and seeing the whole of humanity which is in me. And to see it, I must not be an outsider looking in. Then I do not see it. Then I choose and so on. So, the observer is the observed.

Q: The word art is confusing. You do not know if it is in the right place until you have manoeuvred things and manipulated things.

K: Ah, no sir. When you manoeuvre things, you are acting according to memory.

Q: That is what I am trying to get away from. Art does not mean that, but it means that a lot of times something is right only when it is.

K: The dictionary meaning of art is everything in its right place, where it belongs. So when I listen to a guru, to a priest, to a politician, to my wife, I put everything in its right place. I know how crooked politicians are, so I do not have to think much about it.

Q: That is memory.

K: Of course, but by seeing it I have moved away altogether from memory. Then I act rightly. Sir, this requires a great deal of going into, because what is truth and what is reality? I won't go into all that, please, it takes too long.

Q: I have a question. We began all agreeing about how immoral our society is. And one of your original questions was about how the teacher and the parent go about teaching the child.

K: That is right, sir.

Q: I am wondering what good it does to teach a child or a student that the society is moral or immoral.

K: The child does not know what morality is and what immorality is. You are the educator, I am the parent; I would not talk about the immorality of society. He would not know anything about it. But you and I can talk about it. To him, I would say, 'Find out what it means to listen. Listen to everything on television; listen, find out'. So that the child begins to discover.

Q: I follow this, although I would not encourage them to listen to everything on television. But I wonder about telling someone to listen to the politician. Immorality always comes from society.

K: No, no. The art of listening, sir—not to the politician, to the preacher, to the professor—but how to listen, what it means to listen, not what you are listening to.

You know, it is very difficult to communicate. You and I must know the exact meaning, according to the dictionary, of certain words. Otherwise, you will give one meaning and I will give another. Communication means sharing the exact meaning of the word. Like art. You might say, 'Well, art means painting'. I say, 'No, I do not mean painting, I mean the root meaning of that word, which comes from Greek, Latin, and means this and that'. So we must both understand and share in the meaning of that word. Then we can communicate.

Q: I follow to a certain extent if what we are going to

share is always going to be something that is on the shelf there, or the history of the word.

K: No, but we must begin with sharing the meaning of the word, then we can go much deeper. Take, for instance, the word meditation. All the organized religions and the so-called non-propagandist religions, have some kind of meditation. The meaning of that word is to ponder, to think over. The Hindus come along and say, 'This is the way to meditate. Repeat this, follow this system, practise this, and that is meditation'. I might think that way, and you might think quite the contrary. Therefore we will never be able to communicate. That is all.

So what I am saying is that we must both share in the meaning of the word, which means we must talk together for some days, get to know each other, and the language, the usage of words, how you use them and how I use them, or if I am using words differently from the dictionary meanings. That is why to listen to all this for the first time is very difficult.

CHAPTER 8.

CARING

Krishnamurti (K): Although some of you have been here before, could we begin as though we were doing it for the first time, and go step by step, with a little more concentration, with more attention and more deeply?

If I may, I would like to go into the whole question of education, relationship, and responsibility involved with the teachers, parents and the students. Could we have a really serious dialogue about it, not I talk and you listen, but together? Dialogue, as in the dictionary, means a conversation between two people who are concerned about the same subject, committed to the same subject, with deep, responsible interest. Could we have such a dialogue, not let me talk alone all the time? Then I think we could open up a great deal.

First of all, I would like to have a dialogue about why we educate our children at all; why there is such a thing as a school, college, university; whether these institutions are really destroying the deeper capacities of human beings. Are they cultivating only a very small part of one's life, concerned with the technological development of man and the skills with which he can survive physiologically, totally disregarding the whole psychological field? Could we begin with why we have education, and the need for it? Not that I am against it, please; we are going into it together.

If I had a son or a daughter, would I educate him or her, according to the ordinary sense of the accepted meaning of that word? Would I send them to a school with hundreds of boys and girls, with a teacher who probably has very many students in a class; giving marks, and all the competition; and cultivate the aggressive desire to get ahead of others? That is one part of it. Then there is the cultivation of knowledge, and the use of that knowledge adequately, skilfully, irrespective of ethics. That is another part of it. Another is to go to a university, if one can, and there read a great deal on a special subject and be sufficiently informed to take a degree and enter into the whole rat race. That is what we generally call education.

If I loved my son or daughter, would I put them through all this? Knowing they must have technological knowledge, would I as a concerned parent who loved my children want them to go through all that and enter into a world that is absolutely destructive, that is corrupt, disintegrating, immoral?

Secondly, human beings have really neglected the whole psychological world, which is not only the self but beyond the self, which is the religious world. They have neglected the area of relationship between human beings, concern for correct behaviour, and concern to find out how to live with affection, with care, with love; and also to find out what the meaning of death is. All that is neglected.

If I loved my son, daughter, would I allow this? What shall I do, knowing that they must meet the world, that they have to live in the world, not become a monk or an escapist and go off to Tibet or some idiotic business? They have to meet the world, earn a livelihood. What shall we do?

Could we begin to have a really serious conversation with each other about these matters: the acquisition of knowledge, and the investigation into the area which man has really touched only intellectually? Professors and psychologists and the analysts and the Freudians and the Jungians have touched it, I think, only superficially. Is it possible to enter into the psychological field, which we will call the spiritual, the religious field?

Can we discuss this: first freedom, then knowledge, and third, whether we as parents, teachers, can investigate and so help the student, help our children to investigate into this vast area which man has scarcely touched?

School means leisure. The root meaning of that word, from Greek and Latin, is having leisure to learn. That is the basis of a school. To learn, one must be free to learn; not, 'You have to go to school, you must learn'; do one subject after the other, play, and then come back. Then the student has hardly any leisure, and when he does have leisure, he abuses it. Should we begin with how to create leisure which will not spoil the students, but having leisure, give them the urge to learn? Not only to learn from books and from the educator, but also to learn how to investigate into the great depths of the human mind. Without freedom there is no leisure. Without leisure you cannot learn. So how can we, as educators and parents, see the absolute necessity of having leisure, and of using that leisure properly, rightly, correctly? It can be correct only when there is the sense of freedom. Can we begin with that?

Questioner (Q): Do you think children in the 10 to 13 year-old age group, given this opportunity to have leisure, are innately interested in discovering the deeper things of the mind? I think that they are more interested in discovering the environment around them.

K: Yes, they are more interested in something else, they are not interested in that. As a parent and an educator, what shall we do?

Q: Well, I think that if a child is guided into those areas of interest that are constructive, discovery could build up the momentum to carry him a bit further.

K: We have all been guided. We older people have been guided, shoved into various channels, driven by some social or environmental authority or one's own desire. So we are all slaves of propaganda, of our own desires, which have been cultivated by society, and so on. That is not the problem. If you will excuse me for pointing it out, the problem is, given things as they are, the parents have no desire to learn, they have no leisure. There is the office, the grind; they have no leisure and therefore they are not learning, except in their own fields, technologically. There they get more and more, but they are not learning. So given all these facts as they are, what shall we do? If you guide them, then you are imposing something on them.

Q: Right. I think that it has to be more by example as with a parent.

K: Ah, that means then you become the ideal. They imitate you. Sir, these are all very complex problems.

Q: When a child is 2, 3 or 4 years-old in some families where there are no expectations, they learn faster than in any other years in their lives. There is a kind of free exploration.

K: That means you are not guiding them, you are not becoming an example. If I am an example, then I destroy the whole thing. Therefore there is no compulsion, no propaganda, no example, no authority. Can we, as a group of teachers, parents, really do this, and not theoretically, abstractly? No compulsion, no example, no saying, 'I know better than you do, so listen', which are the ways of the old tradition. We have had examples from the religious teachers down to the local policeman. We have had authorities, specialists of every kind. They have pushed us into all kinds of things. I personally rebel against it. To me that is not spiritual or anything, it is just making imitative machines. So can we together find out not only how to live it as parents in our daily life, but also how to convey the sense of no compulsion, no example, no authority? And yet there must be order. No authority does not mean to do what you like.

Q: But would one then not attempt to impose an outside structure?

K: No, we said no compulsion of any kind.

Q: Not even in the sense of trying to say they are going to talk about it?

K: We all together will find out how to deal with this matter. Not what to do, but to investigate step by step what is involved, not only in our personal life but also with the student. Otherwise this discussion becomes too silly.

Q: You mean most of us as parents have to start a new way of learning.

K: I do not know. You see, you start with an assumption; I do not. I said there is a problem. The problem is that, from everything one has seen in the world, compulsion only breeds fear, conformity, imitation; therefore you may talk of freedom but destroy freedom. No authority, no example—how shall we deal with this? Given these things, how shall we deal with the student?

Q: I think you would have to deal with the student with great respect and trust.

K: Do they trust you? Do they have confidence in you? You see, you are assuming. I am trying to say that here is a problem we have to deal with, not come with a supposition, with a conclusion, with a theory. Here it is. How shall we deal with it? What is my relationship to the student, to the parent, when I say, 'Look, no compulsion of any kind'? It implies no comparison and therefore no imitation, no conformity, and no sense of guiding or example. We have had all that, and produced a monstrous world. So, given the fact that in a school you must not have compulsion, no example, no authority, what shall we do? And yet we must have order, not everybody doing what they like.

Q: I think an atmosphere would have to be created that would allow a change in perception, on both the students' and the parents' parts.

K: Sir, do it. Would you as a parent—I am not talking about you personally, sir—would you see in your daily life that you are not acting according to an example, that there is nothing compulsive about you? Which does not mean you just give up everything. Nothing compulsive in you means for yourself there is no spiritual or any other kind of authority. Except the doctor! Can you do this? If you are going to deal with the student, you cannot pretend and say, 'Look, no authority', and yet you have authority.

Q: Then you would have to watch each other very closely.

K: Madam, here is a problem; what will you do? Have you leisure in your life so as to see that, to investigate into this? Not leisure between two tensions, between two quarrels, between two occupations, but to say, 'I am going to have an hour in which I have nothing to do but to look at this problem, to find out'.

In the ancient system of India, you went to a teacher and you gave your life to that teacher. He would say, 'Now, let us live together and find out'. Together they went at it.

Q: Isn't there great authority and example in that?

K: Of course, example, authority, promises, obedience, kicking. But here we are asking for something totally different. Otherwise we will produce very clever technological machines, or little more than machines, disregarding the whole field which has to be discovered, and which may alter the whole world's work. Otherwise we are just another school. I am sorry, but I would not go near that, I am not interested in that.

Someone says, 'This is your problem: freedom, order, no compulsion, and do not exercise any kind of authority. Work this out, with yourself, with the parents and the school, and with the children'. What will I do? The baby is left in my lap. I have to care for it.

Q: Wouldn't we have to approach it without knowing, then? I mean, we would have to say, 'I do not know what to do'.

K: Will you? You do not know, right? Do you really mean it, or you pretend? Do you say you really do not know, and therefore you are capable of investigating, or do you say, 'I do not know, but tell me about it'?

Q: No, I feel that I really do not know.

K: So if you really do not know, then what will you do? What is the next step? Here is a problem. You have given it to me. I really do not know how to solve it, because I myself have certain authorities, certain examples. I am also very limited in my capacity to investigate, so I say to myself, 'I really do not know how to deal with this'. I am not going to look in any books, I am not going to ask anybody. Are you in that position? Not waiting for an answer.

Q: You mean right now?

K: Why not? Of course. Not tomorrow.

Q: It is frightening to consider, in a sense.

K: If I say, 'I really do not know', not waiting for somebody to tell me or expecting to find an answer, then what has happened to me? Go into it a little bit. You see, we always approach a problem of this kind by saying, 'Yes, this should be done, this should not be done'. We approach from a field which we think is right, with a right answer. We never say to ourselves, 'I do not know what to do with this'.

May I go on a little bit? If I say to myself honestly—without any deception, without any desire to find a solution, with complete integrity—that I really do not know, then I have a new capacity, haven't I? Haven't you?

Q: You are very alert, then.

K: I have suddenly discovered there is a new element which I have not touched before. With all clarity I see what examples have done to mankind. I see what spiritual authority, various forms of authority, have done to mankind. I see that when people talk of freedom, there is no freedom. I see that very clearly, not theoretically. Then this problem is offered to me and I do not know how to work it out. If I say, 'Well, you must have authority because it is worthwhile', if I begin to argue with the problem, then I respond from the old background. But when I see that I cannot find the answer, that I cannot resolve the problem, and say, 'I really do not know', then some other movement takes place. There is no pretence then. I am not clinging to any prejudice, any conclusion, any desire, which always prevent a clear action with a new problem. When I say, 'I do not know', I have discarded all the traditional responses. Will you do that? Has a new element entered into your mind, or are you still playing with the old, traditional responses? When you and I say, 'We do not know', actually, then we are at the same level. Then we can proceed.

From this arises the question: what is the capacity—no, I do not like to use capacity—what is the element, what is the urge that makes one inquire, not theoretically but actually in one's life? Because we are dealing with children, with parents, with teachers, with their life.

Q: Is it a challenge?

K: No. I have gone beyond all challenge. When you challenge me, I generally respond from my old background, as one would to a challenge of a society, of a culture. We are not talking of that. There is no challenge, because I see very clearly that, with a problem which is so complex, any solution according to my background is no answer to that problem. For any challenge, the response will inevitably be according to my background. So I do not accept challenge here. That is very important. It is not because I am challenged that I respond but because the problem is. It is there.

I can go on, but you are not with me, unfortunately.

Q: Well, I think that there is a need in individuals for discovery. Every individual has to operate in a certain environment.

K: Sirs, what are young people interested in? Say, from 10, 15, 20, what are they interested in? Be accurate, not imaginative.

Q: They are interested in how they fit with their peers, with the society they are in, whether they are good or bad, whether they can be best, whether they are going to be a winner or a loser. They are interested in many facets of a society that is not the ideal at all. But I think that there still is a desire to discover that is not from without, but totally from their own sense of wanting to find out about life.

K: You are saying they are really interested to find out about life.

Q: Like a seed in the ground. It might not even be perceived by the person.

K: Take all children, not only in your part of the world but children all over the world. What are children interested in? You say they are interested in discovering what life is. Would you say so? To them life is to enjoy, to play, have fun a great deal; and to study—which is compulsive, frightening because they fear not getting a job. Then sex, their own sexuality and all the pictures and the advertisements and commercials inviting sex, sex, sex. They are also interested in making a good career for themselves—in the army, navy, business, or becoming a gangster, or following this or that guru to make more money. Is this life? This what is happening, sir!

Q: True, that is what happens, but we are trying to find

a way. Not knowing, we are probing. We have to go through what is the basis of a person.

K: According to the analysts, according to Freud, according to all the specialists, a person is conditioned by the parents, by the pot he sits on when he is a baby, and so on. You know all that better than I do. He is a conditioned human being.

I am a parent, I am a teacher, I have a responsibility to the student, to my children, and I see very clearly what is happening. Where there is compulsion of any kind, it becomes imitation, conformity, or fear, and I escape from it into some kind of neurotic business. I see also what examples have done: the so-called highest, the noblest, the hero, the example of the teacher, and so on—conformity, imitation again. All this denies freedom, and therefore I accept authority instinctively.

Now, I say to myself that I do not want my children to grow up in this. I do not know why I have produced them, but I have produced them. I do not want them to enter into a world that is so appalling. I am caught in it, but I do not want them to be caught in it. So I have this problem. And if I respond—please do listen to this—if I respond to that problem according to my prejudice, my background, I am responding according to something which has no value.

So, all that I can say honestly is I really do not know. I have to find a different method, a different approach to the problem, not the old traditional approach. I must find a different approach to this problem. The approach is: can my mind be free to say without any sense of confidence or arrogance, 'I really do not know, I cannot find it'? Can I say I do not know, and therefore I have come to a point when I have leisure. When I say I do not know, I have leisure. All the great scientists—not the government scientists, I am not talking of those, but the really great ones—began by saying, 'I do not know, let's look'. Then how one looks becomes important. I honestly say, 'I do not know'. When I say I do not know, I have no contradiction, I have no examples, I have no authority.

So let us proceed. I do not know. I am waiting. My mind, not being burdened with the past, when it says, 'I do not know', is free to look, isn't it? To look at the problem with fresh eyes. I have children, my own and yours. What shall I do with them? How shall I meet them, knowing that they are already conditioned as much as the parents? Would you dispute the fact that they are conditioned? Obviously they are as conditioned as the parents. They are full of personal responses, personal desires. They have accepted authority. They have said, 'I must be like others'. All the accumulation of society has been dumped on them. How shall I, as an educator, parent, meet that? How do you meet it? What will you do?

Q: Discover where the conditioning lies.

K: No sir. I am asking how you will meet this. You must meet it. This is a problem which you have never faced. It is a problem that demands a non-traditional answer. It demands that you respond to it adequately. It must be correct; it must be true to the problem, not an invented answer. What will you as a parent, as an educator with a lot of children—mine, his, hers, ours—do with them, knowing that they come more or less conditioned? Say there are half a dozen children for whom you are responsible, what will you do?

Q: I guess my response would be to observe them and see what is happening, and then go from there.

K: What need is there for observation? Maybe it is necessary, but I ask why you have to observe.

Sir, may I? If I tread on your toes, forgive me, it is unintended. You are approaching it from the point of view of the [analyst's] couch: 'Lie down, let's observe, let's go into it'. I say you haven't time. The child is already growing up. That is one factor: you have no time. How will you deal with it? There is no time for observation, analysis. Those are all the old methods. You have discarded them. You say, 'I am going to find a different approach to this'. So you discard the whole movement of time. What will you do? You are stripped of everything that you know, and the problem is left to you.

Q: When I show my vulnerability to these students, won't they totally overpower me at that moment? At that moment, they will just do whatever they please.

K: Sir, what is the relationship between you and a man who says, 'I do not know'? That is exactly what is going on now. A man is sitting here who says, 'I really do not know'. And he means, I do not know. What is the relationship between this man who says he does not know and the man who says, 'I have an answer', this, that? What is the relationship between these two people? Isn't it exactly the same with the child, with the student?

Q: So you establish a relationship at that moment.

K: What is my relationship to him?

Q: You are the same at that moment.

K: No. Listen sir. The child is conditioned, and here is a man who says, 'I really do not know how to dissolve this terrible thing which he carries'. What is my relationship to him? What is the relationship now, actually, between you and me? I say honestly, I do not know. I really mean I do not know. And you have answers: 'Observe', 'Don't observe', 'Do this', 'Do that'. What is our relationship?

Q: There isn't any relationship.

K: Wait. Isn't there? Isn't there a relationship between you and me? Then why are you sitting there? Why are you listening to me?

Q: Because we want to learn. We want to discover.

K: We are not dealing with this problem factually, we are dealing theoretically. To me, this is a non-theoretical problem, it is an actual problem. The word actual means accurate, correct; theory, supposition, established order do not come into it at all. It is so. And I am left with that problem, and I do not know what to do. I am not in despair, I am not lost; I do not know.

Q: I have the feeling that we all have the attitude that it is something that is going to happen later. But it is happening right now. I have the feeling that we are all separated here.

K: You are pushing away. Don't you know why you are pushing away from it?

Q: I think we are too removed from it. We think we are involved but we are not.

K: Look, if you are hungry, you want food. Then you do something. Now we are not hungry, we are just talking about it. Therefore you say, 'Well, when I get hungry, I will then do something about it'.

Q: When it is desperate we do something.

K: It is something you have to face! What is the relationship between a man who says, 'Please, I really do not know. I am not pretending. I am not trying to convince you of anything. I really do not know', and you who know? What is the relationship between these two people? Here we are, directly. What is our relationship?

Q: There isn't any.

K: I do not accept that. I will show you. If you do not know and I know—in the sense that I bring out all my answers, all my background, tradition and so on, what actually is our relationship? What takes place?

What is relationship? What does it mean to be related to people? Apart from father, mother, what is relationship? I am not your brother, I am not your wife or your parent, but there is a relationship between us because you are sitting there and I am sitting here talking, concerned with a problem. So we are in a sense related, aren't we? Would you admit that? Now I say, 'I do not know, my friend', and I am saying this from the depth of my heart; there is no pretence, there is no arrogance, none of that. Out of a complete sense of not knowing, I am saying that. And you say, 'Yes, I have to observe the child. I have to look at him.

I have to investigate what kind of conditioning he has, why he is conditioned, how he is conditioned; investigate the parents'. And I am asking you what our relationship is. You say, some say, 'There is no relationship'.

Q: If there are two people who think they know, they are in competition, they are afraid of each other. If one says he does not know, the other one who does know loses his fear. So then he can give up his beliefs, and the two can be without knowing and share something.

K: Yes sir. Is that actually so with you? When you and I are sitting here—I am sorry, I am not being personal, this is very serious to me so I am not pretending, I am not insulting you. I am not investigating you or criticizing, nothing of that kind. Is it a fact to you that you are listening to a man who says he does not know, and you who are listening say, 'Yes, I understand what he means but I am still in the realm of knowing'? You are doing that, so what is our relationship? I am not trying to convince you. I am not directing you. I am not pushing you in any direction. I say, I do not know.

Q: There is space between us, because you are ready to go and I am not.

K: You and I are talking alone, none of these other people exist. I say, 'I do not know'. And you say something or other. I say to you: 'What is our relationship?' You have listened, you have taken the time, you have made tremendous effort. You are here. You have leisure. So what is our relationship? Stick to that one thing. You will see it in a minute.

Q: Well, if one says, 'I know', and one says, 'I do not know', then you have an authority and a non-authority, so there is no learning taking place.

K: So what is our relationship?

Q: It is authority. It is pupil and teacher.

K: Yes sir. Go into it a little more. What is our relationship?

Q: Well, it is fear.

K: Wait. You would not have come from Los Angeles, taken that drive, made all that effort, if you did not want to find out. So take that for granted. Take it also for granted that I am not teaching you anything. Because I do not know. What has happened? Quietly. What has happened?

Q: We have to find out for ourselves.

K: No, there is nothing to find out.

Q: All right. Then there is no movement; you just stand still and listen. My mind must stop.

K: No sir. You are missing something. Just do listen, sir. You have made a tremendous effort to come here. I really mean it, tremendous effort; given up this and that; made effort to come here—out of desire, out of pleasure, out of fear. I am not inquiring into why you came. You have come. And you have listened to this man. And he says, 'I know nothing. I know nothing about this problem. I do not know'. So I say, 'Before you inquire into that problem, what is our relationship?' There must be a relationship, because you have come. You are here. You are listening. There is a communication. So there is a relationship. If you say, 'Go to hell', and walk out, it is finished. So what is it?

Q: Is there a relationship of agreement? We have agreed to come here.

K: No, no, how can you agree with a man who says, 'I do not know'?

Q: There is a relationship of caring.

K: Wait. Go slowly, sir. Caring, what does that mean? He cared to come, took the trouble. So he cared. What does that mean? Not what is he going to do or learn, but the fact of caring. Listen sir. The fact of caring.

Q: Caring about what?

K: No, I am not saying about what.

Q: Just caring.

Q: But isn't that implied? What is it caring about?

K: No, no, I am looking at the pure word itself, not about what.

Q: But there is something implied.

K: You will find out. You are not listening. Please do. You have taken the trouble to come here—driving from Los Angeles to here, the expense. All that indicates not only that you want to listen, but that there is a factor of caring about something. So we have the fact that you care. There is a factor of caring.

Q: Right. Just caring.

K: With care you listened. With care you observed. With care you said, 'Let us see if what this person is saying is true or false'. So you are caught in that extraordinary thing of caring. Otherwise you would not be sitting here. And the man who says, 'I do not know', cares infinitely. So there is a relationship.

Q: Which gives us an intensity to look at the problem.

K: Forget the problem. I am saying care.

Q: And that is the quality that we bring to the children who are going to be in the school.

K: I do not know. I am talking about a man who says he does not know and the man who says, 'I have all the answers to this blasted question'. And you say there is no relationship between the two. I say, 'No, sorry, I do not accept it as easily as that'. I look at it and I say this man has taken infinite trouble to come here, so he must care. Otherwise he would not be here. So the caring is the common factor between the two.

Now push it further. If you really care, then you are out of the realm of tradition. Tradition would say to stay back, not waste time, that it is too dangerous. But you cared. So the common factor is caring. If that is really care, then you care about the problem. Then that very caring means you are looking, finding, not bringing all the old stuff into it.

Q: How does this relate to the student who does not care at all?

K: I will come to that. So, I care and the student does not care. That is a fact. I care infinitely. I really mean it, it is not just words. So I care enormously. So what is my relationship to the student?

Q: Do you have a pre-ordered relationship?

K: No, no, of course it is not pre-ordained. I do not have a blueprint.

Q: Does the child get that feeling of your caring?

K: You are theorizing, you see; that is what I am battling against! I care enormously that my son should not be caught in this world with all the monstrous things that are happening. Because I love my son, I care. And I come to you and I say to you, 'I do not know what to do. You have a school here, you want to do something. What shall we do?'

First, we, the teacher, the parent, have to establish the fact of caring that the boy or girl shall not be like the rest of the world. So I want to see if, as an educator here, you really care; or if it is just a passing whim. Do you really care? Which means are you willing to face the expense, the giving, to care for the children—not for an idea, for the children? That means: do you love the children?

What we are trying to point out is that a new problem has arisen, and you must meet it with a fresh mind, not with a tarnished mind, not with a mind that has all the answers. Here is a problem, here is a crisis which you must meet with a mind that is not cluttered up. And it is not cluttered when you care for something. By caring you have got rid of all the garbage.

So if you say you know what love is, then you really do not know what love is. But if you say, 'I really do not know', you enter a different...

So I have this problem. I have these children, and I care for these children. And I really mean it; I care for these children. I care in the sense that I see what the world is and what they will grow up into, and I care because I love them and want to see that they are not tortured by this world. So what shall I do?

I know. I have looked at it. Do you want me to answer it?

Q: No.

K: Sirs, if you all cared, what would happen? Care with the depth and weight of it! If the parents, the teachers, if all of us grown-up people cared, what would happen?

Q: Society would change totally.

K: Yes sir. Tomorrow we would create... So, what would you do?

Q: At that point, I do not know what to do, but I am certainly going to try to find out.

K: Ah, you have no time to find out. You have no time to find out; the doors are closed. If there was a crisis in front of you, you would not say, 'Let me think about it', would you?

Q: No, you would act.

K: That's just it. You would not sit back and say, 'Let's observe. Let's talk about it'. You would act, do something.

So all people have this problem, and they answer it according to tradition. Every educator in the world has this problem. They say, 'Yes, of course we have this problem. Therefore we have a system of education which we will apply'. But we are saying there is no system, there is no time, there is no observation. It is there in your lap. You have to face that baby; you cannot go to a doctor and find a formula; and you know you cannot kill the baby. So you give all your attention to that; you give undivided, total, complete attention to that. Which you are not doing now.

CHAPTER 9.

TO BE TOTALLY RESPONSIBLE

Krishnamurti (K): We have been discussing the relationship between teachers, parents and the student, because most of us here, parents and teachers, are concerned with the school we have just started. Last time, if I remember rightly, we talked about the question of relationship. What is the relationship between the parent and the teacher, and what is their relationship to the student?

We went into the question of what relationship is, what the implications are of the relationship between parents and children, and of the educator's relationship with the parent and the student. We were concerned with the meaning of the word relationship not only relationship within a small, limited group, but with humanity, with human beings as a whole, because this is an international school. Though it has a very limited number at present, the intention is to bring about an international school connected with the one in England, and those in India where there are a few schools already.

What is relationship? What is the basis or the core of

relationship between human beings, not theoretically, in abstraction, but actually? Because if we do not concern ourselves with what is actual, then we will never be able to grapple with the question. If you merely discuss what relationship is theoretically, then your theory is as good as somebody else's.

In considering what relationship means, we went into the question of care. Care implies affection—we won't use the word love for the moment—attention to the cultivation of the whole mind of the human being, the totality of the human being, not a particular part, not just the cerebral part which memorizes, but holistically with the whole human being; not only the emotional but also the physical, psychological, intellectual and religious aspects.

Is there a relationship between parents and their children? And what is the relationship between the educator and the educated? Taking care means not only while they are young, but right through life; not just giving infinite care when they are babies and then letting that care get less and less by the time they are 15, and after that they are forgotten or they move away completely. We are considering care for the whole of life.

One observes throughout the world that there is infinite care on the part of the mother and the father when their children are 2, 5 or 6, but after that the care lessens. They are handed over to residential and non-residential schools, and the relationship between the educator and the educated becomes compulsive, frightening, based on comparison. And all that is called education. This is what is actually going on in the world.

We are talking of a care, not only while they are very young, but of a care for their bodies, their minds, their whole life, the totality of their activities, not just a segment, so that the children who are so educated do not end up in wars killing each other. We are asking if there is such care on the part of parents and teachers. If it does not exist, then what is the significance of education? Is education merely the cultivation of memory to help the student use facts and knowledge as a very limited, self-centred activity?

We are asking what relationship in life is. Is relationship an abstraction or a reality? We are using the word reality in the sense of actually what it is, not an abstraction of what it should be. The what should be, the ideal, is an abstraction moving away from what is. The moving away becomes an abstraction, the ideal, and so there is never a resolution of what is. We are always pursuing the ideal without ever coming into contact with what is.

We have been asking what the relationship is in a school of this kind between the parent, the student, and the educator. Does the parent merely hand over the children to the educator and forget about them except when meeting them during the holidays or when sending them off to a camp or something? Or does the responsibility of relationship rest with the parent, the teacher, and the student? It is a total movement. That responsibility is care. How do we translate that into action in a school of this kind?

Questioner (Q): I wonder, sir, if in asking this question it is also possible to explore what the responsibility of the student is.

K: What is the responsibility of a student? Has he any responsibility? He comes to a school of this kind, conditioned, frightened, nervous, apprehensive, bringing all the things which he has acquired, consciously or unconsciously, all the impressions, the impositions of society. What is his responsibility? He doesn't even know that word. All he wants is a place where he can find some kind of assurance, some kind of safety, some kind of atmosphere where he feels completely at home. That is what he wants, isn't it? Please, I am not laying down the law. This is a dialogue.

Q: Sir, is the parent's relationship with the child, even up to the age of 5 or 6, perhaps, based on his or her perception of what should be, rather than what is?

K: That is right. Aren't we living on abstractions, on concepts, on ideals, and therefore imprinting on the students, on our children, an abstraction from what is, and trying to live according to that abstraction? So he comes to a school of this kind completely confused. You talk about ideals, yet live totally differently. You say something, and you do not mean it. You tell him not to smoke, and you smoke. He is brought up in a lot of contradictory abstractions and confusions. This is not just my observation. If you observe it throughout the world, this is what is happening. He comes to a school of this kind confused, uncertain, anxious; and you ask him, 'What is your responsibility?' He says, 'What are you talking about?' At least, I would say that if I were a student. I would say, 'What is my responsibility? You have made me. So it is you who are responsible, not I'.

Q: In the process of learning, would not the child come to see that responsibility is not simply a one-way thing?

K: I would not ask the student about his responsibility, but begin with what our responsibility is. As parents, as teachers, what is our responsibility? The word responsibility means, etymologically, to respond. Both responsibility and relationship are based on the words to respond. To respond to what?

Q: To the needs of the child?

K: Do we respond adequately to the needs of the child; that is, give complete security, care and great attention to his demands, to what he feels and so on? Do we give that, or are the parents so occupied with their own problems, with their own self-centred activities that they have very little time for the poor child? If the parents do not respond adequately to the demands of the child, how will the educator respond? What is his position? Can he give total attention to the student? Otherwise he is not a teacher.

We have gone into this question in India very carefully, and also in England at Brockwood and other places: what is the responsibility of an educator? When the parent perhaps has a slight inclination to care for the susceptibilities, the sensitivies of the child but has not the time and does not give attention adequately, then what is the relationship between the parent and the educator? First that must be established, not what the responsibility of the child is. That comes a little later, after having a dialogue with the child. Then we can talk about the child's responsibility.

What is the responsibility of the parent and the teacher in a school of this kind? The parent is as responsible for the child as the educator, because if the educator gives the child great care and attention at school, and then when the student goes home he is not given there an equal amount of care, there is a contradiction. So the student suffers at the end of it, and he prefers to stay with the teacher, and so begins jealousy. All the human tawdriness begins. So if we are concerned with education, one of the important things to be resolved is the relationship between the parent and the educator. Is the parent willing to cooperate with the teacher, or does the parent wash his hands of it and say, 'It is your job'?

Is there such an educator, who is really concerned, who sees his responsibility totally, which means the care of the child's body, the care of his clothes, his taste, the way he lives, talks, the whole of his being? Can we create such a teacher?

Q: A teacher who cares completely about the student.

K: At present such a teacher does not exist. That is a fact. Now, can we together create a teacher who is that? Can you educate yourself or grow to be such a teacher?

Q: We should discuss how to develop in a teacher the ability to respond.

K: Do you as a teacher feel responsible? You are creating a new generation. You are bringing about a different kind of human being in the world, a human being who feels totally responsible for all his activities, who looks at the world not from a limited American or English or any other point of view, but globally. Now, as there are generally no such teachers, can we give the opportunity for a few of us to become such teachers? I think this is very important. Then teaching becomes a sacred profession. It becomes something enormously significant.

Can we move away altogether from abstractions? Abstractions are ideals, concepts, the what should be. The whole structure of thought, which will not face facts, has cultivated a clever, cunning, abstraction called ideals, and tries to live according to those ideals. So can we, here in a school of this kind, live completely with facts and not with abstractions?

What are the implications of abstractions? It is a mind that cannot or will not face facts but moves away from facts into concepts; therefore there is a contradiction between what is and the ideal, and that is how we live. So can we, as responsible teachers, be concerned only with what is? The understanding of what is is enormously important.

Q: Are you saying then that a parent or a teacher might have an idea of what a teacher that really cared is?

K: Yes. If one has heard what we have discussed about the responsibility of the teacher, he can make an abstraction of it, an idea of it, and try to live according to that idea or carry out that idea. Therefore he is always avoiding the fact, the what is, and is cultivating a contradiction not only in himself but also in the student. So there is always a conflict.

Q: But how can one determine what is?

K: That is what we are going into just now. Our culture, our education, our whole Christian, Hindu and Buddhist world and the rest of humanity is based on the cultivation of an ideal and living according to that ideal. So if it is clear that our education, our way of life is based on abstractions and that that creates conflict in life, and if you are concerned with the elimination of conflict, then there would be no abstractions.

Q: In the very talking about it, as we are doing now, we are all dealing with abstractions. We have to speak or think, but what is that moment of getting caught in an abstraction and turning away from the fact? Because to use the word responsibility, or what you have just spoken of, is an abstraction. Those words in our minds are abstractions.

K: No. When you use the word responsibility, the word is not the thing. First let's be clear about that. The word is not the thing. The description is not the described. If you are building a house, you describe it, but that is not the house. So there is the understanding that the word is not the thing. That is the first reality. And when we use the word responsibility, we have to understand the whole content of that word, knowing that the description is not the thing.

So we are dealing not merely with the description, and therefore being caught in the description; we are concerned with the described. One has to be extremely alert or aware that we are not caught in verbal definitions, descriptions, but are concerned with the significance and the meaning that lies behind the word. If I do not have any abstractions—I personally do not—then what takes place? I am dealing with facts, with what is. And I know what is is still not actually what is.

Q: Is it a response?

K: Partly sir. The word responsibility means, as we said, to respond, adequately or inadequately. I realize the difference between the word and the thing, so I am concerned with the thing not with the word. Now, what is it to respond?

I am dealing with what is, not with what should be. The what is says, 'I am really irresponsible because responsibility implies care, attention, love, great committed concern, and I do not have that. I do not pretend to have it. Actually, I do not have it'. So I have found that I do not have the full meaning and implication of that word. Then my action starts not according to an ideal, according to a pattern, a tradition; the mind realizes, sees the fact, that one is really irresponsible. We are irresponsible. I can see why we are irresponsible—because our own self-interest is much greater than concern about the student. In any relationship, self-concern is far greater than the concern for another. That is simple.

Q: Mr Krishnamurti, I am having a lot of difficulty dealing with generalities. I would like to take something very specific like teaching history. It seems to me that most of what we learn at school is a description. In other words, if you take history, when you look at a number of books you will get any number of descriptions about what happened at any given point in history. How can you deal with what is in something like that?

K: I will show it, sir. Modern history is concerned with national states: England is concerned with English history, and America with American, Germany with German, and so on. There is no global history of mankind. If you reject the national histories and are concerned with human, global relationship of man and man, which is also history, then the greater includes the lesser. Therefore it is the responsibility of a first-class educator to see that when he teaches history, he is concerned with global history.

Q: Is it also possible to give the student the perspective that what he is learning is, perhaps, one point of view, but that there are many?

K: Surely. Now let's, if you do not mind, come back to the point that one realizes that one is not totally responsible. I realize, as a parent or an educator, that I am irresponsible. Is that realization a verbal communication or an intellectual grasp, or a total comprehension?

Q: A total comprehension—unarticulated?

K: For the moment, unarticulated.

Q: A feeling?

K: No, do not use the word feeling because that is a rather difficult word. I realize I am totally irresponsible. Is that realization an intellectual realization because you have told me about it?

Q: That would be a belief.

K: A belief, a persuasive argument, and therefore you are still looking at it artificially, superficially. When you rid yourself of the superficiality of hearing a statement and agreeing with it, and see that, it is entirely different from being convinced.

Q: Does that involve seeing an instance of it in yourself, the action of it, and seeing that what is happening is irresponsibility with regard to that?

K: Yes, that is action.

Q: Now, if you see an instance, an incident, is it necessary to see a lot of them?

K: No. Let's go slowly. I realize I am irresponsible. Is that realization a conviction, a persuasion, an impression, a stimulation or is it an actuality? I am hungry. Nobody persuades me, nobody has told me I am hungry. In the same way, is this perception of irresponsibility direct—that is the word—not stimulated, not a propagandistic conviction, but you yourself seeing the fact directly?

Q: Sir, I observe the consequence of my actions, and I see that the child I am dealing with is in pain and that he is unable to relate openly to the world and to his environment. And I observe that I have caused that. Is that my irresponsibility?

K: No, do not use examples, let's get the meaning. What I am trying to get at is the direct perception, and not through an example; not through this, through that, but the direct perception of one's total irresponsibility.

Q: How does one perceive that directly? Either you perceive it in action, which is in a particular instance, or you perceive it as an abstraction.

K: No. Is pain an abstraction? A pain that you have, a toothache or whatever it is, is not an abstraction. Is the realization of irresponsibility an experience, as an individual experiences something? A direct perception is non-personal. And experiences are personal. I may be wrong. We will examine it.

There is a perception that wars will not solve any problem. That is totally impersonal. It is non-nationalistic, non-religious, and so on. Wars, which have been going on for five thousand years, have not solved the problems they set out to solve. That is a perception which has nothing to do with K. Now, if I bring in my personal experience because I have been through a war, that is entirely different from a global perception.

Q: If I were dealing with a youngster or some situation where I realized that I was irresponsible in my actions, what happens in me is that I realize within my brain cells that I was not paying attention to that situation. That is where I discover my irresponsibility; in a specific situation.

K: Do not take any specific example or cases. There is confusion in the world. There is a sense of danger in the world, anxiety, sorrow, pain in human relationship. Do you realize that? I am using the word realize in the sense see it in yourself and therefore in the human being; see it actually, not theoretically.

Do we realize, as a teacher, an educator, that human beings have lived in and created a culture, a civilization which encourages irresponsibility? Do we see the totality of it, not a particular case? If I have a son, I bring him up with infinite care as a baby, educate him through school and college; and then the government calls him up and he goes to Korea or some other place, and he is killed. I say that is utterly irresponsible.

So when we are talking about irresponsibility, I say, 'Am I irresponsible?' Because I am the world. I do not know if you realize that the world is not different from me. The world has created me, and I have created the world. This is a fact, not a theory. The society in which I live is created by human beings, and human beings are a part of me. I am a human being so I am responsible, totally, for all the things that are going on in the world. I am not depressed by it. It is a fact. I am the world.

So do I realize this? Is it not a direct feeling, 'My God, I am that'? Then how do I carry this into action? Because I see I am totally irresponsible, and out of that realization the flowering of responsibility comes. Because I realize I am completely irresponsible, because I have a direct insight, that very perception creates a sense of responsibility.

Q: But that means this is not a conscious act; it involves the whole of the unconscious.

K: What is the unconscious? Apart from what Jung and Freud and all the rest of the psychoanalysts say, what is the unconscious? I am a layman, you are a layman. When you use that word unconscious, what do you mean by it?

Q: The body as it functions mechanically.

K: No, unconscious. When you use the word consciousness, what do you mean by that word? You see, that is why I did not go into that for the moment. What we are trying to say is that the moment I realize I am irresponsible, a new faculty comes into being. The moment I realize I am blind, that I cannot see, I become sensitive to things. But if I pretend I am seeing…

Q: Could it be that you like to see only the irresponsibility in one?

K: No, I am not taking one case. Please, listen to what I am saying. I realize I am totally irresponsible. I believe in God—a theory. I believe in love when really I am anxious, competitive, angry, bitter; and I say, 'I must be noble', when I am ignoble. So all this contributes to a mind that is utterly unstable, and therefore its action is irresponsible. I see that, and out of that perception comes a flowering of responsibility. That is all! A new faculty comes!

I do not know if you have ever tried tying a handkerchief around your eyes for a week to see what happens. I did this. You cultivate sensitivity. You become aware of things of which you were never aware, and so on. In the same way, if one sees this, out of that comes a totally different action.

Now, let's stop there. I realize this and the teacher realizes it in the same way as I do. How shall the two of us convey this to the student and to the parent? Because this school is brought into being by both the parent and teacher, not just by a group of teachers. It is a total coming together of parents and teachers.

So, how shall we convey this to the parent and to the student, knowing the student has come to you totally confused, wanting to do what he wants to do, as a reaction to his home, where it is said, 'Don't do this, do that'? Here you say, 'Be free', and he does what he wants, and therefore becomes irresponsible. Now, how shall we convey to him that he must grow up to be totally responsible? He does not know the meaning of it. How will you create this?

Q: Sir, we create it through our action, our responsible action towards that child.

K: That means, you become the example. The moment you become an example, you become the authority; and when you have authority, he will become another authority. You know the whole business of authorities.

Q: Is it by the example that is being shown, or is it by the truly responsible action he senses in the other person?

K: I am asking you: if you are a teacher how will you help him, educate him to have this feeling of total responsibility, to nature, to animals, to human beings, to the whales, to everything in life? That means responsibility for his behaviour, for the way he thinks, the way he feels. How will you convey this to him, educate him? Come on, it's your job.

Q: By showing him what his responsibility is and what the implications of his actions are.

K: At that age, do you think he would listen to you? Does he know what you are talking about? Responsibility—he is frightened by that word.

Q: Sir, can I go back for a moment to what you were talking about before? Caring totally.

K: Does the parent care totally, or are you asking the teacher to care totally?

Q: I was asking the teacher to care totally.

K: Which means what? The parents say, 'Please. You help him to care totally and I will stand by and watch'.

Q: Well, the parent must also.

K: That is what I am asking, sir. Is the parent involved with the teacher to see that his children are cared for totally?

Q: Of course.

K: Therefore I am asking, if the parent and if the educator say, 'It is our responsibility to see that the student has this quality, this beauty of caring', what will they do?

Q: First get the parent and the child to accept their irresponsibility.

K: We have been through that, sir. No, don't burden the poor child with that heavy word, responsibility. My question was: knowing the child is frightened, anxious, looking for somebody to say, 'Look, it is all right old boy, be quiet', and so on, how will the educator convey or help to bring about this quality of infinite care? What will you do?

Q: Sir, he will respond to the child. In the relationship between the parent, the child and the teacher there are an infinite number of instances where the teacher has to respond. Aren't we talking about the quality of the response to that child?

K: No, I am asking you a question. You already have children here. You feel the utter necessity and importance of helping them to have the feeling of total responsibility. What will you do?

Q: In principle, don't I have to be totally responsible?

K: But you are not. You are learning by talking. We have had leisure this afternoon from 2:30, and we are learning. You see the beauty of it, and work. But you cannot put that burden on the child. He has enough burdens already, so do not add another one. I am asking the teacher what he will do.

Q: He moves the child not by giving an example in the overt sense, saying, 'Oh, look at me, I am so responsible, be like me'. But will he unconsciously absorb the good?

K: Do not use the word unconscious because that has a different significance.

Q: If the child feels something from a responsible adult, a parent or a teacher, he doesn't think of imitating him but his own sense of responsibility grows, without it being labelled or without it being the result of copying something.

K: Look, we have spent an hour on this question. You have listened to it. You have listened to the question of responsibility and relationship. As human beings we are not responsible and we have realized that we are irresponsible, and the realization is not artificial, intellectual, or theoretical but an actual fact. Now, hasn't this created an atmosphere? I am asking a very simple question. You have listened to all this and you feel, 'Yes, that is perfectly true'. And therefore isn't there a certain atmosphere in this?

Q: Yes. Definitely.

K: Now, what happens? Can we create this atmosphere into which the child comes?

Q: It has already been created.

K: Ah, a few of us create this atmosphere, in the sense that we have talked about it. We have gone into it, we have looked at it; we have torn it apart; we have, you know, drunk it, tasted it, and smelt it, slept with it. Therefore there is an atmosphere, isn't there? And the child comes into the atmosphere. I do not tell him about being responsible. He would say, 'What are you talking about?' But he has come into an atmosphere in which there is the feeling that you care infinitely, that the teacher cares infinitely. You have done the first action then!

Q: And then the second action is that this atmosphere must extend to the home.

K: If it is not at home he says, 'I prefer to stay at school'. So we have created an atmosphere, which is immensely important. After all, a perfect home, sir, a house that is perfectly harmonious, in the depth, the size and the proportions, has a peculiar austerity of its own. You do not have to say, 'This is an austere home'. It is there!

So when a child enters into this, he is bound to feel, 'By Jove, here are people who do care'. He may not put it that way, he may not articulate it, but probably he feels it. Then you can begin. Then you talk about clothes, food, taste; everything begins.

Q: Sir, would you say something about the word austere as you are using it?

K: Yes. The word actually, in the dictionary, means ash, the ashes of fire. That is, you have burnt everything out in yourself. The original meaning is that you become an ash because you have denied sex, you have denied drink, you have denied the world. You have denied, not gone into it, understood it. You have denied, therefore you have made yourself into ash. We are not using the word austere in that monkish sense of the word, but totally differently, which is that it comes out of harmony. When there is complete harmony in oneself, that itself is austere in the sense there is beauty in austerity.

Q: Is that in any sense related to necessity, the mere necessity?

K: Necessity for what?

Q: Say, for living, what one needs for living.

K: Yes, lots of people have done this, they will have only what is necessary, nothing else, just one pair of shoes; or in India a loincloth, one robe. But we are not talking of such austerity. We are talking of an austerity of a mind that has understood the whole significance of life and lived.

So can we create a certain atmosphere? Not consciously, not deliberately saying we are going to create it by incense and ringing a bell and all the rest of it; but because we see the truth that one's existence has been lived irresponsibly; then that very perception is responsibility. That creates an extraordinary sense of stability.

That means that those of us who are teachers in the school have to have a dialogue about this. Not say, 'You are irresponsible', or 'You are responsible'. That becomes too childish and personal, embittering and narrow. So have a dialogue about the reality and the implications of irresponsibility and responsibility. Have a dialogue about it, talk about it, go into it, as we are doing now.

You see, in that atmosphere is implied that you care about what he eats, what kind of clothes he puts on, how he walks, the manner of his speech, the way he looks at people. All that is implied in his taste. Because you are concerned about him or her, if there is that feeling, they will sense it immediately: 'Here are a group of people who really care what I am, what I do, what I think'. Can we create such a school here where the parents and the teachers are responsible, together?

Also we ought to talk about freedom; whether freedom is an abstraction made by one who is in prison, or if there is freedom per se, in itself. That is implied in a school of this kind because without freedom you cannot learn. As we said, the meaning of the word school comes from the word leisure, to have leisure. When you have leisure then you may be able to learn. That is the meaning of a school: a place where you have leisure to learn. And you cannot have leisure if you are not free to learn. You may have leisure but you may have innumerable problems. Then that leisure is used to escape from the problems.

Because human beings are burdened with a thousand problems, they have no leisure, and therefore they are not learning. So here we are giving an opportunity not only for the student but also for the older people like us, who have gathered together, because we have leisure and are therefore learning together. Now, can there be freedom for the student to learn? Or will he misuse that freedom and therefore not learn?

One has to go very deeply into the question of what freedom is, because freedom is one of the most important things in life. What is freedom? Can there be freedom when there is authority? And without authority, doesn't freedom lead to disorder? And if there is no authority, will there be chaos and therefore the denial of freedom? In a school of this kind, freedom is absolutely necessary.

Q: How does that relate to rules?

K: What is the relationship between rules and freedom? Why do you have rules? You must get up at nine o'clock or at six o'clock, have meals at one o'clock. Rules about silence, all kinds of rules in a school. Why do you have rules?

Q: As a group of people living together, there must be a certain amount of basic, simple order.

K: Why do you have rules, sir? Rules exist in order to have order, which means you are dealing with a group of people who are disorderly. You impose rules in order to make them orderly. That means you are denying freedom. Now, can there be order with freedom? How will you bring about order without rules, and yet have freedom?

Q: Can there be freedom with disorder?

K: No, of course not. But that is what we are trained, educated for; to have freedom in disorder.

Here are a group of children and teachers. How will you bring about order without rules, without compulsion, without threats, rewards? Let's work at it, let's find out. Let's learn about it. Here are young children who are disorderly; life in their homes is disorderly. How will you help them to be orderly?

CHAPTER 10.

HOW WILL YOU EDUCATE THE STUDENT NOT TO BE HURT?

Krishnamurti (K): In a school of this kind, the parents and the teachers are in a relationship of responsibility, not the teachers alone. Can there be a responsibility on the part of the parents and the teachers to bring about a different kind of mind, a different kind of human being who is not incessantly in conflict within himself and so with society and with the world?

Is it at all possible through education to bring about an intelligence which will guide the student right through life? The word intelligence is a rather difficult word. It means to read between the lines: in Latin inter legere; legere, to read, inter, between. Not only that, but also to have deep insight into what you are reading; and to have a deep insight into the observer, into the mind or the character or the person who is reading. Can we, in a school of this kind, bring about such intelligence, which will meet every kind of challenge naturally, and respond adequately, not neurotically, not disjointedly or fragmentarily, but wholly?

What kind of education should the parents and the educator demand? If you had a child here, what kind of education would you want him or her to have? In a disintegrating world this is really a very important question. If I had a son or a daughter here, what kind of education would I want for him or her? Is it merely to cultivate knowledge only in a part of the brain, and to disregard the entirety of the mind, and so meet life always fragmentarily?

Is it possible to cultivate the totality of a human being? Surely that is what we mean by education, not merely to give information to be used skilfully in daily life as knowledge. That is only a very small part. But when one disregards or neglects the whole psychological, moral, ethical, aesthetic, religious side of life, then one is breaking life into many fragments. And those fragmentary activities bring about a great deal of suffering, conflict, and misery.

Please, this is not a talk by the speaker, it is a dialogue, a conversation between us all. So please don't let me be the only person who speaks. Let us all share in this discussion.

To put it differently, we are dealing with human beings, not with a European mind or an American mind, but a global mind. We human beings are not the result of a particular provincial, political state, we are the result of the total endeavour of man whether he lives in India, Japan, Russia, in Europe or here. We are the result of all that. We are the result of the total historical movement of man, not of a particular country. I think that is fairly obvious.

Can there be an education which will give the student a global outlook, a feeling of responsibility for the whole of humanity, not just for his little family? This is very important, because our study of history or literature and so on is always from a local and not from a world outlook. How shall we educate your son or daughter in this school to have a feeling of responsibility for the whole of mankind? Is that too big a job? Is that demanding too much, not only of ourselves but of the student? Won't you discuss this?

Questioner (Q): I think the feeling of compassion that I have seen a child have for an animal is where it begins; and then the child expands that feeling to other things.

K: Do you know what the word compassion means?

Q: Reaching out toward?

K: No, it is not emotion. To me emotion, sentimentality has nothing whatsoever to do with compassion. Compassion implies passion for all things; not for one particular group, but for all living things. Very few people have that kind of compassion. They have a lot of romantic sentimentality about animals, about human beings, but sentiment is really quite dangerous because it leads to ruthlessness. So compassion is something that comes out of suffering, not out of sentiment. The word passion has its root in suffering. But we human beings have evaded or escaped or tried to run away from suffering. Religions have offered escapes. We have never faced suffering, remained with suffering, not trying to evade it or explain it away or seek comfort, but being with it totally. When one is totally with it, out of that comes compassion, passion.

Is it possible for a human being to live without moving away from a fact, whether it be fear, pleasure, suffering, or any form of human reactions; to remain with it completely, without any movement away from it? We are trained, educated to move away from the actuality, from what is.

Our problem is that, as human beings, we are conditioned to act in a very limited area, to think along a particular line; and such activity has not ended wars, has not made man intelligent. I am using the word intelligent in its right sense according to the dictionary, not according to my interpretation of what intelligence should be. Can the educator, the parent and so the student, help each other to bring about a global intelligence?

Q: To bring about this global intelligence, isn't it necessary to see our relationship to all other living things?

K: Yes sir. What is our relationship with human beings? What do we mean by that word related? What does it mean to be related? Is relationship based on pleasure, on convenience, on comfort? Is relationship being lonely and being attached to another? When relationship has a motive from loneliness, seeking comfort, dependency, attachment, would you call all that relationship—or exploiting each other? Can we have a relationship which is not exploiting?

Q: Are you asking, as we sit here in this room, if we have a relationship that is not exploiting?

K: No, first we are trying to understand what that word means to all of us; whether what we call relationship is a subliminal, romantic attachment, or an attachment born out of loneliness, frustration, longing to be loved, longing to have companionship, longing to be with somebody who will help us. We must be clear, when we use the word relationship, what we mean by it. Otherwise you will interpret it one way and another will modify what you say. We want to find out the truth of relationship, the truth, the full significance of that word.

Q: Doesn't it primarily mean contact?

K: Yes, contact. Relationship means not only physical contact, sexually and in other ways, but also psychological contact—psychological, intellectual, emotional—that is, total contact. When we use the word relationship, what do we exactly mean by it? In our daily contacts, in our actual daily movement of life, not in abstraction, when we use the word relationship, what do we mean by it? When we say, 'I am related to my wife, my husband, my children', what does it all mean? To you as a human being, to each one of us here, what does relationship mean?

Q: It seems to be life, simply life.

K: Sir, I am not married, but if I say 'my wife' what do I mean? What does my relationship to her mean?

Q: Doesn't it mean interaction between human beings and other creatures, or else the universe, on a wider scale?

K: Interaction between myself, my wife and my children, my neighbour, and with the cosmos, with the universe. Interaction. What is my interaction between myself and my neighbour, between myself and my wife, and the universe? Have I an interaction? Is to inter-act to be inter-related? Or is it always from a centre which is constantly being strengthened, and acting from that centre?

When we talk of relationship, what is the interaction between two people? Sir, I know you; I met you several times: last year, the year before, and recently, quite often. What is my relationship to you, and what is your relationship to me? I have known you. You have known me. Do I know you actually or do I have a picture of you or an image of you, and it is that image meeting you? From what you said, what you did not say, what was said between the lines, and so on, I have a picture of you, just as you have a picture of me. So, what is the interaction between us?

Q: Usually it is an interaction between pictures.

K: That is it: interaction between memories, between words, between pictures; which is so unreal.

Q: But there is something a lot deeper than that.

K: Wait. To go deeply you must first see the surface. Can we look at each other—wife, husband, whatever it is—without a single picture? Then we can have a relationship that is not at a verbal level, not from a recent or old memory, but a totally different movement takes place. Can we do this?

Please, this is not group therapy. I have a horror of all that.

Actually, as two human beings talking about relationship, unless you and I are both free from image-making, picture-making, then you and I have no actual relationship.

Now, suppose that, as a Hindu with all the superstitions, all the training of tradition and a thousand things involved in being a Hindu, I am conditioned by that. If I have this ancient, traditional conditioning, from that I respond, I interact. Unless I am free from that immense weight of tradition, which is picture-making on a grand scale, I have no relationship with you at all.

Q: By being free of that, do you mean that as long as I think that I am my conditioning or I am my mind...

K: Aren't you your conditioning? Are you different from your conditioning?

Q: I experience something different from all that. That kind of goes along on the top.

K: Ah, no, just a minute, sir. We must go a little slowly on this matter. Are you different from your conditioning?

Q: I do not see how.

K: I do not see either, but people think they are different from their conditioning.

This brings us to a much more complex question: is the observer different from the observed? If the observer is different from the observed then he says, 'I am different from my conditioning'. Then you have to examine who the observer is. Isn't the observer the memories, the judgments, the traditions, all that, which is the conditioning itself?

Q: But what about intelligence?

K: Intelligence, as we said, is the capacity to read between the lines. We are doing that now. And not only reading between the lines, but also having an insight into a statement instantly, to see if it is false or true. The capacity of instant perception of what is true or of what is not true is intelligence.

Q: Sir, earlier you used the term psychological interaction. Would you say that this instant perception of action and intelligence is without any psychological superstructure at all?

K: Of course, otherwise it is not intelligence.

Q: Yes. So that is the same as the observer, the whole psychological structure.

K: Obviously.

Q: But if I identify myself with intelligence and my experience of intelligence, isn't that different from conditioning?

K: No. When you identify with intelligence, who are "you" to identify with it?

Q: Well, in that step I lose myself.

K: Who is "yourself" to lose?

Q: Well, that is the conditioned part.

K: So when you are unconditioned you are intelligent—there is intelligence, not you become intelligent.

Q: Yes.

K: So let's come back. We are talking of relationship. Relationship means to be in complete contact with another human being. Complete: intellectually, morally, spiritually—if I may use that word spiritually—the total, non-fragmented human being in contact with another non-fragmented human being. Otherwise there is no relationship. Is that possible when we live in a world where everyone gets hurt? Is it possible, first, not to be hurt—which creates resistance and enclosing within oneself? You know, all the problems of hurt, which may be one of the reasons why there is no actual relationship completely with another human being. So, is it possible not to be hurt?

If I had a son in the school, I would be concerned tremendously to help him never to be hurt. I do not mean physically, I mean psychologically. Is that possible?

Q: Sir, what happens to him when he goes out into the world then, where he obviously will be hurt? Or is that relevant?

K: It is relevant because if he can understand what hurt is, if he can understand the whole meaning of it and what it implies—the resistance, the hardness, the bitterness, all that is implied in that hurt—if he understands that and how not to be hurt, ever, then he can face the world. So how will I educate the student, my son, my daughter, to see that he or she is never hurt? How would you proceed? It is part of their education. What would you do? Go on, look at it. What shall I do? There are two things involved: how to prevent being hurt and what to do with a human being who is already hurt. What will you do? How will you educate the student in the school not to be hurt?

Q: First of all, inquire into what it is that gets hurt and also what the nature of the hurt is, what it means to be hurt.

K: In school, the teacher calls me a fool. I am hurt. Another boy says, 'You are an ass'. I am hurt. When I am compared with my elder brother who is much cleverer than I, and somebody says, 'You must be like that', I am hurt. The process of relationship with each other is a movement in hurt.

Q: It means comparison.

K: As long as there is comparison, there must be hurt.

Q: Hurt being a sensation which arises out of a sense of inadequacy, smallness, in comparison.

K: Yes, smallness. When you compare me with somebody, you are denying me. You are denying my existence, my life, you deny me. When you say I must be like my elder brother, you are destroying me. It is so simple.

Q: Then it is not the comparison itself which denies, but the ideal.

K: No, it is the whole fact of comparison, not the ideal. It is the fact of comparison. When you compare me with somebody else, aren't you putting me into a straitjacket? You are not concerned with me, you are concerned with the person you think is very clever. Can I help the student never to compare himself with anybody?

Q: So if that denial is non-acceptance, that student must be fully accepted for who he is.

K: I must help him never to compare himself with another. The educator must be aware, fully, never to put him in that position—comparing marks. We tried not giving marks in India, but you have to keep an eye on how the student is getting along; parents demand a report from the teacher about what the student is doing. The whole system is based on that.

Q: So the comparison is not with somebody else but with where they were three months ago.

K: Yes. So that means the educator must be extraordinarily aware of all this.

Psychological hurts prevent a total relationship. You are responsible for these students. Can we see that they understand the meaning of hurt and are never hurt? What is it that gets hurt? When you call me a fool, why should I be hurt? Because I have an image that I am not a fool. You are hurting the image which I have created about myself.

Q: Is it not the case that one gets hurt, not simply because there is an image, but because one clings to the image?

K: You are that image. You are not different from the image.

Q: Is it the ego and the whole process of conditioning that is hurt?

K: Let's be very simple. You have an image about yourself, and if I call you an ugly name you are hurt. You are that image, aren't you? You are not different from that image. You have created an image about yourself, and that image gets hurt. Can you prevent a student from creating an image about himself? Do you see how difficult it is? Because all the world says, 'You are that image; build an image about yourself, otherwise you are nobody. You are going to be the President of the United States; you are going to be a great man', and so on. So you create a tremendous image about yourself. Then someone comes along and says, 'Don't be an ass', and you shrink. So can we, through the right kind of education, prevent image-forming in the student? Can we help the student not to create an image about himself? Otherwise he is going to get hurt all his life. And the consequences of being hurt are what the modern word is: violence, desire to hurt people in the name of peace, all the ugliness that comes.

You are the educator, I am the student. Can you help me not to be hurt? Not through romantic nonsense: 'Oh darling, don't be hurt', and all that. That means nothing. Can you help me never to be hurt? That means you as the educator have to understand what it means. Also it means that you have no image about yourself either, which means that, in talking with the student, you are helping yourself and the student not to create images. So in a dialogue with the student you are helping him not to have an image, because you yourself will not have an image.

Knowing that you do have an image and by talking about it, you are pulling it to shreds.

Q: I have trouble seeing a state where you do not have any image.

K: Forgive me for saying so, but you are making an abstraction of it. Suppose I have an image. I want to understand that, not what is going to happen if I do not have an image. That is a supposition, that is an abstraction. I will face that, I will understand it when it comes. First I realise I have an image and realise that image is myself, that the image is not different from me, and that as long as there is an image, there will be hurt. So my question is: is it possible not to create images?

Both of us must understand that as long as you and I have an image about ourselves, we will get hurt. That is a law, like gravity. Is that image created by society or by yourself? Please, go slowly with this. Do not answer it yet. I am asking if you have created it or society has created it. Society being education, parents, the economic structure, politics, the environment. Has the environment created the image or you yourself have created the image, apart from the environment? Or you are the environment? You are not different from society, because you are the result of your parents' parents' parents' parents, who have created the society of which you are a part. The culture in which you live is your culture; you are not different from that culture. So you, society with you and the environment, everything has created that picture through education: you go to school and they say, 'You are better than your brother'. 'You must be as well-off as your uncle'. So you create an image. Society, with your help, has created this image. And this image is not different from you. You are that.

The next question is: is it possible to be free of that image?

Q: To be free of it without analysing the implications of it.

K: I make a statement. It may be false or it may be true. I say to you: 'There is an image in you, and you are that image'. Do you see instantly the fact you are that, or must you analyse it and through analysis come to a deduction, and agree with that deduction, and say, 'Yes, I agree with you'? That is totally different from direct perception seeing the truth that you are that. Do you see instantly that you are the image, that the image is not different from you?

We are talking over together being hurt. That is one part of it. Tremendous things are involved. One part of it is that from childhood we are hurt—through comparison, through the ideal: 'You must be that'; or through asserting, 'You are inferior'. All that creates hurts. If I have been hurt, is it possible now to wipe away that hurt completely without leaving a mark?

Q: Probably not. One is inured to these things, has had these experiences in life.

K: So we become hardened to it, which means we put up with it. I have been hurt and there is no answer to this, so I will live with it. I do not want to live with it.

Q: What else can we do?

K: Go into it. I will show it to you. I do not want to live with my hurts, become accustomed to them, accept them, be habituated to them. To me it is like having a wound all my life. I do not want to have a wound all my life. What shall I do? You see, you accept it. I will not accept it. What shall I do? There are two things involved. First, I have been hurt. That is one problem. And the other is never to be hurt.

I have an image of myself. That image is not created by someone but is the result of human conditioning. So I have that image—there is that image. That image is not different from me. That image is me. That is absolutely so, factual. Then what shall I do? There are two things, I said. One is not to be hurt ever again, and what shall I do with the hurts that I have accumulated?

I have an image about myself. That image has been put into my mind through generations and generations of human minds. That image is in me, and I have created part of that image. So I am that image. That gets hurt. This is an obvious fact. The psyche gets hurt. The psyche is the image. That image has been hurt and does not know what to do with it. So it gets hardened, resists, builds a wall around itself. That is one thing. The other is, never to be hurt again. You are the educators. What shall we do with the children who have been hurt by their parents, by their society, by everybody? What will you do?

Q: Can you explain the process of hurt to children?

K: No, they are too small. They are too small; but they are already hurt. What will you do with the child who has been hurt psychologically, as most children are?

I cannot reason with him, can I? He is too small. I cannot persuade him, not really, because that is too silly. I cannot say to him, 'I am not hurt, therefore do not be hurt'. That means another hurt. The example is another form of hurt. So what shall I do? No example, no coercion, no saying, 'My darling, do not be hurt'. All that has no meaning, so what shall I do?

Do I, as a parent, as an educator, understand the meaning of it, the significance of it, the depth of it, the brutality of it, the viciousness of people hurting him? Do I, as a parent, as an educator, understand the depth of that, the meaning of that? It means that I may be hurt, and I want to understand the whole process of being hurt in myself. I must have an insight into it. I must read between the lines. So I will have a dialogue with the child, showing him what hurt means, how people become bitter, sharp, violent, withdrawn, neurotic. I will point all this out to him, discuss with him. Because I am working on myself first; when I say to another, 'Do not be hurt. I am not hurt', it is not just words. I have understood it; I have gone into it; I have seen the full meaning of it. So I will talk to him.

Speech has its own magic. Speech, when it is true, has an effect. But it must be true. The truth is that I have understood it. I am not hurt by anybody because I have no image about myself. Because I have no image about myself, then what I say about hurt is truth.

In talking over with the student and with you, I and the teachers will see that we understand the depth of all this. In talking over with you, I am looking at the picture in myself. I become tremendously aware of the picture which is hurt. The picture is myself. As long as there is a picture as "me" there will be hurt. I see it absolutely, not relatively, because I am aware of the whole significance, the full meaning of being hurt; not through analysis but by direct perception.

Q: If one talked to a 6 year-old, could he understand?

K: I would not talk to him about hurt, because he would not understand, poor chap. I would talk to him about picture-making, about how everybody makes pictures about themselves. He would understand that. I invent a lot of ways to tell him because I am tremendously concerned that he should not be hurt. Then I will find a way to tell him how animals kill each other. I would bring everything into that, historically.

Is it possible when I am hurt to wipe that away, not get used to it, not get hardened? Is that possible?

You have been hurt, haven't you? Everybody is hurt. Why do you tolerate it? Why do you hold it?

Q: I do not know what to do with it.

K: Yes. So, it is immensely important for you not to be hurt. What will you do?

Q: I do not know what to do but investigate it.

K: Ah, no. It is tremendously important not to be hurt, because if you are hurt you cannot see flowers, you cannot see beauty. You cannot see anything if you are hurt. You cannot see the blue sky, you cannot see colour—anything—if you are hurt. So it is absolutely important to find out how to end this hurt. What will you do?

Q: If it is an image of ourselves that is hurt, then stop the image-making.

K: Then why haven't you done it?

Q: I don't know.

K: Is it laziness? Is it laziness, indifference, callousness, forgetful indulgence in something else?

Q: I think in my case it could be all of those.

K: What would you do if it was a life and death matter?

Q: I would fight and it would not really do any good.

K: No, that is right.

Q: But that is what we do.

K: That is what you do, fight; and you jolly well know that is not going to do anything. So what will you do, knowing all this?

Q: Would it be necessary to understand, to see the whole process, to observe the whole process?

K: I have explained that the image is created by society; the society is you; the society is the result of a thousand generations of human beings, and that human being is you. That human being holds an image which gets hurt. That is a fact.

Q: Why are we so reluctant to drop the image? We hold onto the images so long.

K: I am asking why you have not dropped them.

Q: What entity is going to drop the image? Who is it that is going drop it?

K: That is just it, sir. They are all talking of dropping the image, fighting the image, getting rid of the image, pushing it down the drain. But who is the thing that flushes it?

Q: Isn't it the image? Is there anything other than the image?

K: No. It is another image that says, 'I must get rid of that'. So what will you do?

Q: Is there an activity of forgiveness? Is there such a thing as forgiveness?

K: I can forgive you, but the hurt remains. I can say, 'Poor chap, poor lady, I did not mean that'. But I am already crying. Please do not play with words.

Q: Have you a solution to this?

K: Of course, otherwise I would not be talking about it. It is not a solution.

Now, will you listen to me for two minutes? Listen. Do you know what it means to listen? To pay complete attention. Otherwise you cannot listen. If you are teaching me something, I must not be looking out of the window. But if you are teaching me, and I do, you say, 'All right, look out of the window completely. Finish with it, and then listen to me'. Now, will you listen to me in that way, completely. Will you? Completely, not interpreting, not translating, not being caught in words, not asking, 'What do you mean by that word?' or saying that the word means something else, and so on, and so on. To pay complete attention implies that there is no centre from which you are attending, there is no centre from which you are listening; there is only complete attention.

Now, pay complete attention to your image. Is there an image?

Q: There isn't any image.

K: If I pay complete attention, there is no image. It is only when I do not pay attention that I get hurt. Look, when you listen to music, you are attending, aren't you? And there is no centre from which you are attending. You do not say, 'Ah, I heard Toscanini play it much better'. Or, 'I prefer Beethoven to Mozart'. You don't do that. You listen, don't you?

Q: Ideally, yes.

K: Then is there a centre from which you are listening? No. Right? Now, with that same attention, look at the image. Is there an image then?

It is only when there is no attention that the image-formation takes place. Have you got it? That is all. That means that when you give complete attention, the past hurt and the future hurts are non-existent.

So can you live life that way? Do you get it, sir?

Q: Yes, I get it, it's great. (Laughs)

K: No, it is not a trick.

Q: But isn't that what relationship is, too?

K: Can there be such attention in relationship? That means that with my wife, I do not know my wife. Therefore I am looking at life afresh every moment. When I listen to Beethoven, Mozart, Bach, I listen. And so when my wife says something, I listen. When she says something silly, I listen. There is no image-making when there is attention. If you grasp that once, the thing is over. It is my laziness, my inattention that makes the image.

So I want to teach my students to listen, to pay attention. How shall I help them to pay attention when they are totally inattentive all their life? They have no responsibility for attention, they do not know what it means. They have only been trained to concentrate on a book: 'Don't look out the window, look at the book'. So they are trained to concentrate, not to attend.

Q: You said they are trained to concentrate, but we cannot train them to be attentive.

K: No. So I am going to help them. I will show it to you. Do you see the difference between concentration and attention? In attention there is no effort. In concentration there is a division between the entity who wants to concentrate and the entity that says, 'I want to look out of the window'. So there is a vast difference between concentration and attention. Now, I want to help the student to attend. What shall I do?

Q: Be attentive to him.

K: I attend to him, but he does not know what it means. Please follow it. Don't have an answer, please, let's investigate. You understand, sir, investigate! What shall I do when the child is inattentive, has learned the trick of concentration and does not know what real attention means? What shall I do? How shall I help him?

Q: Investigate inattention with him.

K: He won't even know about investigation. Sir, take your child. What will you do? The students who come, what will you do with them? You want to help them to attend, to see the full meaning of that marvellous word.

Q: Has it something to do with the interest, with the passion that can be generated over the thing that is being attended to?

K: Then I am interested in one thing and not interested in the other; therefore I pay attention to one thing and not to the other. Therefore I only know what interests me, which has nothing to do with attention. I want him to find out, learn, what attention means.

Q: But don't we have to find out what the child is interested in at that time?

K: I have just explained, sir. If the child is interested, he pays attention. If he is interested in a toy, he is paying attention to the toy. Remove the toy, he loses attention. We are talking of attention per se, in itself, not about being attracted by something which interests him.

Q: And you think that is possible for a child?

K: We will find out. I will show it to you. I do not know, but I will show it to you. To me, to attend is the most marvellous thing. The word itself rings a bell of great depth. I want to convey this to the child. How shall I do it, knowing he is inattentive, has learnt a little bit of concentration, but is not interested in what we are talking about? What shall I do?

Well sir? Don't be silent, find out.

Q: I wish I could say. I do not know.

K: You have to find out. You cannot say, 'I do not know', and leave it at that. You have to work. Now, go on, move. What shall I do?

(Pause)

Do you have it? I have it. I have an answer. You see, we are used to fragmentary interests. I am interested in mathematics; I am interested in painting; I am interested in building something. That is fragmentary. Can there be non-fragmentary interest?

Q: Does that mean to be interested in everything?

K: No. Ah! You see how you translate. Through negation you come to the positive. We have fragmentary interests—boys interested in cooking, girls interested in something or other—and nothing else. I am asking if there can be a non-fragmentary interest, which is not saying be interested in everything.

Q: I do not see the difference.

K: Sir, you see the fact that children have fragmentary interests, and therefore their life is fragmentary interests. But we are educating them to be interested in the whole of life. So, as their interests are fragmentary, ask if there is a non-fragmentary interest. It is a negative question. If I pursue the negative, I come to the positive. Not begin with the positive.

Q: Non-fragmentary interest has a lot of depth to it.

K: That is what I want to establish first, a non-fragmentary interest. And I am going to find out what the movement of fragmentary interest does, and the movement of non-fragmentary interest, the one and the other. The movement of fragmentary interest makes a fragmentary life: I am a businessman and nothing else; I am an artist and nothing else. We live and function in little compartments. I see that the result of that is a fragmentary world, a fragmentary human being. I love my wife, and go out and kill people. So I see that a fragmentary interest makes for a fragmentary life. I do not know what non-fragmentary existence is. I know the one, but I do not know the other. So what shall I do?

Q: If you were paying total attention all the time, there is no fragmentary interest.

K: Of course, but do look at it. Isn't interest always fragmentary? Interest is always fragmentary. Where there is interest, it must be fragmentary. Is there activity which is not interest?

Q: Attention.

K: No, do not go off into attention. We said, fragmentary interest; and we also said interest must always be fragmentary. Because if I am interested, I cannot be interested in the whole. I do not know what the whole is. Is there an action which is not vested in interest, which is not born of interest? Personal interest, interest in an ideal, interest in a society, interest in improvement, interest in this, that—all those are fragmentary. Is there an action which is whole, which is not based on or have its roots in interest?

Q: Is that attention?

Q: Would it be perception?

K: No, break away from the words because otherwise you will not find something new.

Q: Would we act without interest?

K: I am asking that without interest. I do not have interest in finding an answer. That is why I am going to find it.

Q: But is it possible to act without interest?

K: I am doing it.

Q: You are not interested in finding an answer?

K: No. Put the question without wanting an answer. Are you putting it from an interest or are you putting it like dropping a stone in a pond?

Q: Are you saying the point is the question, not the answer?

K: I am asking you. I see that all interest is fragmentary. Interest in biology, interest in physics, interest in music, interest in literature, interest in business, interest in God, interest in this, that, the other—they are all fragmentary. That means that where there is interest it must bring fragmentation. I have discovered something new. So I want to find out if there is an answer to the question: is there an action which is totally devoid of all interest, and therefore is whole? I must find an action which is totally devoid of all personal, environmental concerns. Isn't there one? There is. I will show it to you.

Sir, from where do you put a question? From what state of mind do you put a question? I have said all interest is fragmentary; which is logical, which is explainable; you can see it. And I am asking: is there an action which is not based on interest? Is there an action which has no roots in interest? From what state of mind do you put that question? Is your mind interested in finding an answer? If you put that question with a mind that is interested in finding an answer, it is still acting fragmentarily. So you will not find the answer. So I am asking: from what state do you put that question?

Q: A clear mind?

K: No, watch it, sir. Put it to yourself. I am asking you: have you an interest in finding an answer? Are you putting the question because you are interested in finding an answer? If you are interested in that, then your answer will be fragmentary. So I am asking you from what state of mind, or state of whatever it is, you put the question. Is it out of silence? I do not want to lead you.

Q: Sir, if you are putting it from the point of view of interest in the question, is that the same thing?

K: That is still the same.

Q: But I am faced with a question.

K: I am asking you from what quality of mind, from what state of mind, from what background of mind you put that question. Is there a blank, quiet, still, emptiness, silence, a sense of putting the question and seeing what is coming out of it because you are asking totally without interest?

Q: Then why do you ask it?

K: I have led up to it. Do not ask why I have asked. I have said all interest is fragmentary. If I put the question with interest, the response will be fragmentary. Is there an answer, a response, which is total, whole, not fragmentary?

I have put that question with complete not-knowing. I do not know. So I have no interest, personal or otherwise, in what comes out of it. Something is being born out of it, a new flower. There is a flowering taking place because there is no interest. I wonder if you are meeting me. Come on!

Q: Are you saying the interest is attached to the particular, therefore it is fragmentary?

K: Yes. We have been through all that.

Q: So you are asking the question without any multiplicity of pieces.

K: Yes, I am asking you from what state of mind you put that question. It is so simple you do not see it!

Q: There is no answer.

K: You put the question. Your interest has been in this or that. Therefore the interest has made life fragmentary. And we discover that where there is interest, there must be fragmentary activity. And if there is no interest, what is the action?

Q: Whole.

K: Whole.

Q: There is pure action.

K: Whole.

Q: Yes.

K: That is all. Then your action from the whole is total, everywhere. That means everywhere you are exercising complete intelligence. You see, we always live in fragmentary activity. We do not know what total activity is. We do not know it because we are interested in fragments. If I see the nature of interest, and that it is fragmentary, I see, I have an insight; that is the truth. Therefore there is an action which is whole. Can I live that action through my daily life?

CHAPTER 11.

CAN I HELP THE STUDENT TO LISTEN?

Krishnamurti (K): The last time we met here we were talking about how important it is to prevent students or children from being hurt. We said that most people, grown-ups as well as little children, are deeply hurt by all kinds of things: by their parents, by their fellow students, other children, by society. The whole structure of modern living, apparently, hurts people very deeply, whether consciously or unconsciously. Is it at all possible to prevent children from being hurt? We went into that fairly deeply.

From that question arises another important problem. There is such disorder in the world, chaos really, great turbulence, uncertainty, a vast disorder inwardly and outwardly. Now, how do we bring about, without compulsion, without punishment, without reward, a sense of order in children?

I was once travelling from Bombay, a four-hour train journey, and in the same compartment there was an American mother with two children. During those four hours, the two children raised hell. They were in the racks, they were under the seats and running up and down shouting, until the mother turned to us and said, 'Can't you do something with them?' (Laughter) That is the state of the world, generally, wanting somebody else to do something about bringing order. So, in a school of this kind, where parents, the educators and the students are working together, how can we help the students to bring about order in their lives and around them every day?

Traditional discipline based on reward and punishment, on authority, is disappearing. Without authority, without compulsion, reward and punishment, how would we help the student to understand what order is, and willingly to cooperate to bring about that order? Without compulsion, without any form of threat, reward, that whole cycle, how would you do it?

What does order mean, or discipline? What would you say order is? The word discipline has its root meaning in disciple, one who is willing to learn. The idea of discipline is the act of learning; not complying, not imitating, not conforming, not subjugating, but the movement of learning all the time. That brings about its own order. That is the original Latin meaning of the word discipline. How would we, the parent, the educator, help to bring about order—if you think order is necessary? What is order? Order and discipline basically mean the same thing. One cannot learn if there is no order, which means leisure, and willingness to cooperate with the educator in the act of learning.

Order means, generally, traditionally, conformity to a pattern. That is what we generally mean by order, whether it is the order established by a society, by a parent, by a church, or by a religion: the sense of disciplined conformity to a pattern. Most intelligent people reject that. We do not want to conform to a pattern set by somebody else, by society or by the priests; conform to an authority in the hope that there will be order. All that has been rejected. Order is not conformity to a pattern established by a society, by a church, by a parent, by an establishment. That is authority. One intelligently puts that aside, understanding that the whole nature of authority implies compulsion, conformity, imitation, example, and therefore there is always fear. If that does not free the mind of grown-up people as well as children, what then is order? If we can understand that, perhaps we will be able to help the student to bring it about. If there is no freedom, can there be order? All these questions are involved.

Freedom generally has been understood, especially in America, as permissiveness; allowing the adolescent and the older generation to do exactly what they want to do: individual enterprise, individual freedom, individual ambition, individual success, individual fulfilment in whatever pleasure, the whole of that. To choose. Is that freedom? Not theoretically, not in abstraction, but actually in our life. We have done that. The grown-ups, the past generations or the present generation do exactly what they want; and we bring up our children in the same atmosphere, to do what they want. Is that freedom?

Questioner (Q): It seems that there is another meaning for the word conformity. If I were going to look at that carefully, it would seem to me that it says "formed together".

K: Form, plus con meaning with: "formed together".

Q: And that brings to mind that conforming then would be an alignment of purposes among individuals.

K: Like the totalitarian states conform, form together, cooperate together.

Q: Not with an authority, but together. If you could get a group's purposes aligned so that they are all moving together, then that is different.

K: Wait. How do we move together? Is that based on an idea, on a principle, or on a belief or an end? Sir, how do we, you and I, a few of us, cooperate? Which is, go together: cooperate, work together.

Q: If it is a belief or an idea or a concept, it is outside of what is happening right now. In fact it is happening right in this room, right now. We are forming around this.

K: Which means not around a person, not around a belief, not around an authority or an ideal. That means freedom. How am I as an educator to convey this to my students? They are used to non-conformity. They are used to doing what they want. They will not even want to listen to me. So how are we going to deal with this?

Q: I still do not know what disorder is.

K: What is the nature of disorder? Conflict, contradiction, in speech, in thought and in action. Saying one thing, doing something else. So there is always a contradiction. Would you say order is total harmony in which there is no contradiction?

Q: Yes.

K: No, wait, be careful. A definition is not the fact. I can define, but the definition is not the reality.

I say to myself: as a human being, as an educator, is my life, which is the life of the world, harmonious, non-contradictory? If it is not, how can I convey it to the student? I become a hypocrite, saying, 'You must have order, you must have harmony', and in myself I lead an utterly disorderly, inharmonious life. The student will say, 'Please go and jump in the lake'. He will not actually say that, he is too polite, or frightened. So how do we deal with this question?

In the Asiatic world, people are very docile. It is their tradition. You must not go against the elders. You must listen to them. When they talk, you must keep quiet. It is very easy to deal with them; you tell them what to do and they will do it. But when I go to the schools in India, I say, 'Do not do that. Let's examine what you are doing, what it leads to—death'. Conformity ultimately leads to death, for civilization, in every way.

Now what shall we do? The parents are disorderly, contradictory in themselves. They smoke and tell the child, 'Do not smoke'. It is a simple fact. They drink, and so on. The parents are contradictory, inharmonious, conforming to a pattern which they think is right, and so on, and they bring up their children that way. So how shall we deal with this?

Q: It seems obvious: be an example.

K: That means what? Imitation. I do not want to imitate anybody. Why should I? You may be God on earth, why should I imitate you? Not that I am vain or superior. We have lived on imitation. There are dozens of examples: religious examples, heroic examples, thousands of them. Why should I copy anybody? That is what is happening. So you are not an example. One cannot be an example; it is too immature to make myself an example for somebody when I am not whole myself, when I lead a double, crooked, disorderly life, pretending to be something I am not. So, no example, no authority, no conformity, in the usual sense.

This goes contrary to everything that has been established. All the religions have said: there is the example, follow, obey, accept, believe. The Jesuits vow absolute obedience to the authority without equivocation; whatever the authority says, they accept. And we have that spirit in us, vaguely, somewhere. If you intelligently understand the whole business of that and put it all aside, then how shall we educate ourselves and the children to live a totally orderly, harmonious life?

The Greeks talked about it. The Greeks had an idea of harmony between the mind and the body—physical harmony, first. The perfect Greek sculpture is totally outwardly completely harmonious. But is an outward appearance harmony, or is harmony something very, very deep which needs to be inquired into, lived, found? If we want to find out, to educate children and ourselves to live an orderly life, what is the movement towards that?

We live a contradictory life. That is understood. That is a fact. That is doing one thing, thinking another; the ideal and the factual. There is a contradiction: 'I must be that', when I am not that. So it is a dualistic, opposing, contradictory existence. How does this arise? Does it arise because of man and woman; light and dark; night and day, the good and the bad? Man, woman, sex and all that is a normal, natural process of life, but not the contradiction.

Q: Didn't it arise from not living in the now?

K: You are saying it arises because we do not know how to live in the now. Let's inquire into it. What do you mean by the now?

Q: I mean what is happening at this present moment.

K: What is happening at the present moment? Is it unrelated to the past and to the future? These are very complex questions. Is the present, the now, something totally unrelated to time? I am sorry to make it difficult. It is not. I am asking. That means time must have a stop, and only then there is the now.

Q: It seems to me that the disharmony that we were talking about, or the conflict, comes from a separation, which creates the duality.

K: We are asking how it came about in human beings. Why is it that a human being—it doesn't matter where he lives—has this sense of duality: the ideal and the fact; the good and the bad; dark and light? This has been going on for five thousand years and more. In the caves of Lascaux they have found the same dualistic conflicts, opposing elements from 25,000 or 30,000 years ago. I want to find out how it arose. I will not dwell too long on it because I lose my energy to get deeper if I merely dissect, analyse. So I am asking myself and I am asking you, if I may, why one lives a contradictory, opposing, dualistic life, the "me" and the "not-me", we and they, and so on. I want to investigate into that because I am concerned as an educator, as a parent, to see if I can help my children, my son, my daughter, and the student not to live that way, to be free of conflict. So I have to find out how the human mind has accepted this.

Q: In psychology there is an area of study called object-formation, which says the child gradually learns to differentiate himself from everything around him.

K: Sir, would you say that where there is division there must be conflict?

Q: Yes, there is opposition.

K: There is opposition. So division is the factor of conflict: the Arab and the Jew, the Muslim and the Hindu, the Christian and the non-Christian. How did this arise?

Q: Division is one of the first things we learn, and we keep learning it. As a very tiny infant, what is over there is different from my crib or my bottle.

K: Yes, let's leave the children, for the moment. Are you aware that you live in contradiction? Be simple, sir. One does.

Q: Yes.

K: How did it arise? Do not go back to the child. How did it arise in you?

Q: Through ideals. Because one wishes one could be other than one actually is.

K: Why? I have the ideal and the fact. Why have I established the ideal?

Q: You sense that there is something greater than you, and you want to attain that.

K: Yes. Why? Proceed, go into it. Why have I said the ideal is much greater than the fact?

Q: Sometimes it is obvious. Sometimes you can see it very clearly. One feels inadequate.

K: There are two factors: the what is, the actual, and the ideal, non-actual. How did this come into being? Why have I divided the ideal, the non-factual, and the fact, what is? If you knew how to deal with the fact, would you invent an ideal?

Q: No.

K: There it is! If I knew what to do with what I have, I would not look to the future, I would be acting with what I have. Because I do not know what to do with what is, and am afraid of not knowing what to do with what is, I then proceed to project an abstraction which I call the ideal.

You said inadequacy. I am inadequate to deal with the

fact, with what is in my hand or in my heart, in my mind. I do not know how to deal with it, what to do with it; therefore I am frightened about it and escape to something which is non-actual.

Q: Why don't we know how to deal with it?

Q: Well, it is quite obvious.

K: No, in life, not intellectually, not verbally. In daily life, can I deal with the fact and put away all abstractions—the ideal, what should be, and what should not be, the whole structure of human thought which has created a network of escapes?

Q: Well, isn't this concern with harmony and order also an escape?

K: No. I am saying, let's begin with this. We live a contradictory life. We live a life of conflict. We live a life of division. We live a life of opposition. This is our daily life. Wars, the communists, the socialists, the whole thing is that. Now coming very much nearer, I say to myself: why is there this contradiction in me as a human being? If I can resolve that, I have resolved the human problem. So I am not concerned personally; I am concerned because I am a human being; whether in India, America, Russia, it is a human problem.

So I see that one of the factors of division is that I do not know how to deal with what is; and not knowing what to do with it, being inadequate, incapable, I am afraid of it and move away from it. So I realize that the escape from what is is one of the major factors of contradiction. So now, in my life, there is no escaping. Finished! When I see something, it is finished. Therefore I am now faced with what is.

Q: Which is the contradiction, the division.

K: With what is—no contradiction. There is no contradiction. I am a liar. I am greedy. There is no question of not being greedy, not lying, that I must tell the truth. There is only the fact that I am greedy.

Q: And then you are passing judgment upon that.

K: No, I have accepted the fact that I am frightened, greedy, envious, jealous; whatever it is. That is a fact. Before, I moved away from it and said, 'I must not be jealous', or I found reasons for being jealous, justifying it, and so on. Now I have stopped doing that. Therefore I have this thing, which is that I am jealous, antagonistic, I feel angry, all that. Now, can I deal with it? Not in terms of going beyond it, which again is an escape; can I meet it and dissolve it? Which is not an opposition.

Take violence. Human beings are apparently violent by nature. Which I question, but it does not matter. Human beings are at present violent. And there has been a cult of non-violence: Gandhi, and in the Western world Martin Luther King, and so on. Can I deal with that violence with a mind that is not dualistic?

Q: Not seeking non-violence.

K: No, I have no non-violence in my mind because I see that is an escape; I see that leads to all kinds of mischievous things. When the fact is this, dealing with something else is non-factual. So my mind is free from the opposite. Is your mind free from the opposite when we are discussing this, or is it merely theoretical?

Q: I have labelled the thing which I am as "violent".

K: Just wait. Keep to that. We will go into it. I have removed from my mind the opposite, the non-violent, the conflict to be non-violent. I have removed from my mind the whole sense and the structure and the nature of the opposite, the duality, the artificial invention of a thought. All that is gone.

Q: By accepting the negative.

K: No, that is what I have. I do not have non-violence.

Q: Yes.

K: Now, is your mind like that? Can you look at the fact with eyes which are not coloured with the opposites? This is very important, because quite a different action takes place.

I am violent. When I move away from that into an abstraction because I am not adequate to deal with it, I am wasting energy. I am wasting energy by running away, avoiding the fact. When I do not run away, I have energy. Oh, please; have you got it? Do not agree. This is not a matter of agreement. Do you have that energy which comes when there is no escape?

Then the problem arises: why have I—why has the mind—named it violence? There is anger, violence. Violence implies anger, jealousy, hatred. All that is involved in that one word for the moment. We will include all those things in that word. When the feeling of anger arises, why have I called it anger, or why have I called something violence or jealousy? Why have I named it? The moment I have a feeling, I name it. Why? Look at what I am doing. I have named a feeling as hurt, or jealousy. I have named it almost instantly. How does this movement take place?

You will see it in a minute. We are investigating together. It is not that I am investigating and you are just listening; together we are looking into it. Therefore it is yours as well as mine.

Q: Does one actually name it or do you just live it and act it out?

K: Oh yes, you name it. Don't you name it?

Q: In the midst of it I would say not.

K: At the second, you do not. A moment, a second later, you name it.

Q: Yes.

K: You slap me and I get angry. I get emotional; adrenaline and all the rest of it works and I am stirred. And I say, 'I must not be angry, how stupid of me'.

Q: You check yourself.

K: I check myself or let myself go. I am asking why this naming process goes on.

Q: Doesn't the mind try to sort things out?

K: Do look into it in yourself, you will see it in a minute. Has the word become more important than the feeling?

Q: Do you actually name it if it is a familiar feeling? When it is unfamiliar, you think, 'What is it?' and then you start plucking words.

K: I am taking something with which we are very familiar. That is, anger, jealousy, greed, envy, hatred are all actions of some form of violence. And I say to myself that when the feeling arises, at that second there is no naming. The whole thing is absorbed in it. But a second later, I name it. So I am asking: is the naming process a form of asserting? The word is stronger than the feeling. Or I name it so as to recognize it. Go slowly. That is, I have had that feeling before and I have named it before and I recognize it now and call it by the same name. So that strengthens the present feeling, by naming it.

Q: Doesn't that also enable you to reject it? Because you say, 'Yes, it is the same as that thing I remember'.

K: Yes, you reject it, but that requires much more alertness. Please go with me, you are going off. So there is this factor. The word may have become stronger; the word is not the thing, but we have made the thing the word. The word door is not the door. But with us, by naming a thing, the word has assumed the feeling. I am asking you why we name it, not at the second of a feeling, but a moment, a second later?

Q: Is it recognition of the fact in order to reject it?

K: No. We have not come to the state of rejection.

Q: At the first moment, the feeling is direct and personal. At the second, we put it into the cultural system in which we were brought up, because then we think that we know how to deal with it.

K: That is what I am coming to. We hope by naming it, by recognizing it, to deal with it. But we do not because we have mistaken the thing for the word. Please see that.

Wait, let me get this myself. (Laughs) I have just said something. Yes, I have it right. That is right. The word becomes stronger, and then through the word we hope to deal with the fact. But when we know the word is not the thing, then the word does not play an important part. Wife, the word, is not the wife; but the word wife has become tremendously important. The word. So when I recognize that the word is not the thing, is not the fact, then the word, the naming loses its vitality.

Q: Isn't it also that the mind likes to deal with the familiar?

K: Yes. It is familiar: I am angry. You accept it, and I accept it, and get on with it. But if I want to find out why I name it, why there is this dualistic existence, I have to face the fact that the word has become tremendously important. And not being adequate to deal with the fact, I have created an abstraction and escaped from the fact. With a non-abstractive way of living, I would be dealing with fact. Then the word is not the thing, so I have gathered energy, the mind has tremendous energy now. The word is not the thing, therefore I am no longer caught in the word. There is energy because there is no escape into abstraction, into an ideal. So there is energy.

When there is no movement away from what is, then you can deal with it because you have energy. It is the lack of energy that has made you move away from the fact. Do you see it? Look at it carefully, please.

I have no energy, and I do not know how to deal with a fact. Therefore I lazily wander away, accept the tradition of moving away, the culture of moving away. When I do not move away, I have the energy to meet with it. When I have that energy, is there anger?

Q: That anger then is the energy.

K: There is only energy, which I have misused as anger. I escaped from it, dissipated that energy in abstractions and in words. But when I have that energy, where is anger?

Q: You used the word laziness. That is a key word it would seem, because it is much easier not to look at the thing that you have used a symbol for.

K: Yes. That means the mind that is lazy, the mind that is traditional, the mind that is used to traditional escapes, does not know how to deal with it, and creates the problem of duality. Then it is caught in it and goes on and on and on and on. When there is no escape, when there is no cage of words to be caught in, then you have energy; and when the mind has energy there is no dualistic response.

Now, to come back. I want to convey this to my son, daughter, to my student. How shall I do this? It is my responsibility. I am responsible for that student, for my son, daughter, to see that he or she lives without conflict.

How shall I proceed? This very complex explanation is not the fact; the description is not the described, and so on. To me this is an absolute reality, truth. For me this is life. Personally I have no conflict; I have never had it, and I think it is stupid to have conflicts. So, knowing my son, my daughter, the students, and the grown-up parents are living in conflict and are comparing, what shall I do? How will you deal with this as a parent? You have children, how will you deal with this?

Q: Sir, could we talk about cooperation?

K: The child does not know what it means. Cooperate with whom?

Q: With other students. With teachers, with parents.

K: What for? Why should I? How will you convey to your son or daughter, to the student, not to be in conflict? How will you educate them when they have lived in conflict, when the environment is in conflict? Their parents, everything around them is in conflict. You say, 'Look, do not live in conflict'. They say, 'What the dickens are you talking about?'

Q: You have to undo the damage that has been done, but how?

K: The damage has been done; but in the learning of something which is new, the damage might be wiped out. In the learning of the new, the old disappears.

The educator is in conflict and the student is in conflict. They are not perfect, harmonious human beings. That would be a different matter. But the educator and the educated are both in conflict. Now, how will you deal with this? Both are ignorant. How will each one help the other to dispel this ignorance?

Q: Part of the conflict, perhaps, is due to the fact that you have an ideal.

K: Sir, you have an ideal, the educator has an ideal, the student has an ideal. How will you dispel this idealism so as to face the fact? How will you set about it?

Q: By having an environment where the student and the teacher can inquire together.

K: Here we are. Let's take that. I am the teacher, educator, you are the student. How shall I help you? I want to help, as an educator. You are my student and you are violent, you have idealism, you have escaped from the fact. So has the educator. Now, suppose this takes place. How will we help each other to dispel this?

Q: By facing the fact of ourselves. The elder person can do it but I do not know if a child can.

K: You listened to me, didn't you? Can you help the student to listen? You came here. You had leisure. You wanted to find out, were curious or serious. So can you help the student to listen?

Q: But in order to listen, one must be interested.

K: No. Must you have interest to listen? Look, I want to tell you something. I say, 'Please, do listen to what I have to say'. There is no interest. My very urgency, my very demand makes you listen, doesn't it? I say to you, 'I love you', and you listen, because that interests you. That means something to you. So can I help the student to listen? Not to what I am going to say, but to learn the act of listening.

I would help my student to learn how to listen. Just to listen. I would keep at it. I would help him to listen; 'Listen to birds, and then listen to me; because I am your educator, I am your teacher. I love you, I have to help you to live a life which has no relation to conflict'. So I say to him, 'First learn listening'.

Sirs, why do you listen to what I am saying? Tell me why you listen.

Q: I want to understand.

K: You want to understand what?

Q: The problem we are talking about.

K: What problem? I am asking you. What problem?

Q: To understand ourselves.

K: You came here, you listened to this man, to K, because you think he might help you to understand. You think. He might not, he might. So you came here to find out what he has to say about yourself, yourself being the world, the human being. You are not separate from the rest of humanity. So you have come to listen, to find out what K has to say about yourself, who is the human. That means you want to listen to find out. First listen. Did you?

Q: No.

K: That is all. And you expect the child to listen to you? (Laughs) So why don't we listen? Please, this is really a very important point. Why don't we listen?

Q: We are too busy answering.

K: That is, you listen but you have an argument already prepared to meet it: opinions, judgments, comparisons. You say, 'Yes, I have heard this man say that', and you are off. So you take all the trouble to come here, and never listen. So, how shall I help you to listen?

Q: You cannot.

K: Ah! Do not say 'you cannot'; then you are finished. My interest, urgency is to help you to listen! I have intense urgency, passion. I have! To help you to listen. Now, how shall I help you to listen? I have the passion, I have the fire. I feel intensely about this. I do, factually. And you say, 'Yes, you are nice, what you said is quite right, but somebody else has said that'; and, 'What time is it?' 'I am sorry, I am a bit tired'. 'I overate, I am sleepy'. 'It is a lovely day, I would like to be on the mountain'. You are not listening. How shall I help you to listen?

Q: I was just going to say, isn't it up to us now? I think you have done your part.

K: No, no, I have not done my part. My part is right to the end. If I said to you passionately, 'I love you', would you listen?

Q: Probably not.

K: I am asking you. If there is something in you which

is alive, passionate, and I appeal to that, you would listen then.

Q: Naturally. Of course.

K: If you have a terrible disease, and I say to you, 'Look, I will show you something that will help', you would put your heart into it. Here there is no reward. There is no panacea. There is nothing that I am giving you and that you are taking. We are sharing. Therefore you become slack. I do all the investigation; you listen and say, 'Yes, I agree. He is quite right'.

It is my responsibility to help you to listen. And if I felt that same responsibility towards the child, towards the student, I would talk to him, have a dialogue about listening; take him out for a walk; at the table, any time. I would say, 'Listen to that bird; listen to what I am saying'. My passion will help. It is the lukewarm person who will do nothing for the boy.

Q: Isn't it simpler for a child to listen to the sounds of nature and the world around him, than it is for an adult who is inured to so many other things?

K: Yes, to listen. I want to listen; not to Beethoven and Mozart or the birds, I want to listen to what my thoughts are doing, what I am feeling, what I look at, how I look at it. I am listening to find out what is happening to my mind. Can't I do that? Why do I live in this conflict? I am listening for the answer. I am listening to find a hole through which I can look.

Q: Don't you think many of us listen, and are awake in the

night and are confused? We think, and we try to find an answer.

K: Ah, no, no. You try to find an answer, but I do not try to find an answer. I put the question that the question is going to answer. But if I say, 'Well, I will put the question', and look around, look around, I have lost it.

Q: It seems to me that all I can do is live that intensity. I cannot make the child listen to me. All I can do is live. All I can do is act out my own intensity, my own care.

K: That is, I am awfully interested—not interested—it is my deep concern to find out a way of living in which there is no conflict. That is my deep, serious, passionate concern. And I say, 'All right, I am going to deal only with fact and nothing else'. The fact is not the word, the fact is not the escape. So I have the energy. When I have the energy, the fact has no importance, it is gone.

But how am I as an educator going to deal with the student? On Monday some of you are going to meet them. What will you do? Knowing they do not want to listen to you, that they are full of play, mischief, will do anything else, chase butterflies and so on, what will you do? How will you meet them?

Q: I think I would start by really listening to them.

K: Yes. What are they saying? What are you listening to? This endless chatter about nothing? You think the children have a lot to give to you.

Q: Yes, I do.

K: So you are the child, and so it is the child helping the child; the blind leading the blind. I met several parents in Europe and in India. They said, 'Oh, children will give you a lot'. I said, 'What?' They said, 'Listen to them'. I said, 'What are you listening to? What are you learning from children? To be childish? To be innocent? To play?'

Q: But if you do not really listen to them at any time, how can you get them to listen to you?

K: You say you would listen to them. I ask why, and you say they will give you something. And I said, 'What will they give? If you are going to receive something from them, how can you educate them?'

Q: How about if what you receive is their attention?

K: We always want to receive, we want to take, we want to learn from somebody. The whole of mankind's beginning is in you. You are the repository of the whole of human existence. Your mind is the result of a million years of human existence. So if you know how to read that, why do you have to receive anything from anybody? If one realizes, not verbally but actually, that one is the result of the total human existence—all its endeavour, suffering, misery, confusion, agony, happiness, joy, the endless suffering of humans—that it is all in you, you have to face that and resolve it. There it is, it is all there.

So what will you teachers do on Monday morning? I am sorry to rub this in, or ask, or insist. What will you do? Oh, don't keep silent, please, I am going to keep at you.

Q: Sir, can we begin by simply attending to what is, and continually pointing it to them?

K: Then you become a nag.

Q: You had better be there! (Laughter)

K: No, you see, if I am there, the children would pay attention because I am new. They would pay a little attention because my face is different. They would say, 'Oh, who is he?'

So what will you do, sirs? Those children are your responsibility. You cannot be silent, you have to act.

Q: Right now I do not know what I would do then.

K: I am your student. What will you do? I live in conflict. You know what children are.

Q: If one could create an atmosphere where they would feel that they could discuss these things, where there would be an open interchange between the students…

K: Yes, but how do you create that atmosphere?

Q: By sharing your existence with them?

K: That is, by having a dialogue with them sometimes, but how long will that take? We are grown-up people. We come to a very simple fact, that we do not know how to deal with the fact; therefore we run away. And it took how long to show you something? And you are grown up, willing to listen. And the children are not willing to listen to you. They want to play, they want to climb a tree, they want to do this or that. They say, 'Oh, this is a bore. I will have to put up with it', and grumbling they come.

Q: Have you an answer to this?

K: You see? I would know how to if I were there; I would know how to deal with it.

We respond adequately when there is a great crisis, don't we? That is a fact, isn't it? Given a great crisis, I respond. I have to respond, because it is such a tremendous crisis. I forget about my family, forget myself, and respond to it. People respond to kill in a war: they forget about themselves and want to go out and kill somebody.

Now, we have a crisis here. The crisis is that you have children who will not listen to you, who are totally disorderly, in the deep sense. They are used to being compelled, and so on, and you are meeting a crisis, which is that you want to bring great, deep order. That is the crisis. It is not just words, it is absolutely necessary in a school of this kind. There must be total order—in their speech, in their walk, in the way they eat, the way they dress—order right through their being. That is a crisis. How will you meet it? You will meet it if that crisis is really a crisis. You will not just say, 'Well, I will meet it the day after tomorrow'. The crisis is there.

If my son dies, it is a tremendous crisis. And I respond either by escaping, by all kinds of idiocies, or I respond to the thing that demands my complete attention. Because death is an enormous thing, I respond to the challenge to my highest.

So here is a crisis. The crisis between two people: the student and the educator. If it is not a crisis to you, you will say, 'Well, hasta manana'.

We have asked the architects to build something

extraordinarily beautiful here, something that will endure, that is timeless. That is a crisis for them if they take it seriously, and because of that crisis they will produce something. When you say, 'I love you', to a woman, and she refuses to look at you, it is a crisis.

Q: Sir, can we admit that we simply do not know what to do, and just start looking?

K: Actually, when you say you do not know, it is a crisis, isn't it? It is a tremendous crisis for someone to say, 'I really do not know'. If it is a crisis, the very not-knowing produces something. Whenever I talk, I really do not know. Whether I talk in public or in private interviews, I do not know. Therefore something new comes out each time.

Q: What is going to happen to those children on Monday morning?

K: We are going to find out.

CHAPTER 12.

TO BE DILIGENT IS TO GIVE COMPLETE ATTENTION

Krishnamurti (K): Will somebody set the ball rolling or shall I?

Questioner (Q): Sir, you said on several occasions that if you had the responsibility of teaching young children, you would begin by helping them to understand something about the art of listening. I wonder if we might not discuss something of that today.

K: The art of listening, the art of seeing, and the art of learning, the three arts.

Q: It seems to me that when you speak of listening perhaps you mean something a little bit different by it than what we ordinarily mean when we use the word. For us, one is listening if one can recall what was said and repeat it back.

K: That is only a part of it, isn't it? The word art comes from Latin, meaning to put everything in its right place, where it belongs. Everything, not just one or two things but the totality of existence; to put everything in that existence in its right place; that is the meaning I am giving the word. The dictionary says: to put everything in its right place.

Now, how can we help each other, and so the student, to listen? Not only to confirm the information that you have given him, to re-state it in his own words, but also to go behind the words. Because for most of us words become all-important. If we can use words cleverly, it is astonishing; one becomes an orator, without much depth. Listen to words, because speech is very important. Listen to words and communicate exactly what those words mean to each other. Not only the dictionary meaning, but the meaning that is contained, say, in a word like wisdom. You cannot talk to children about wisdom, but a word like wisdom has tremendous depth to it. Listen to that word, and get the depth of that meaning.

Q: Which is something more than the dictionary meaning.

K: Of course. One has to go into the whole of what wisdom is.

The art of listening, it seems to me, if I may point out, is to listen totally, with all your senses. We were talking about it the other day with someone. When you see a mountain or the sea or a beautiful tree, do you see it with all your senses or only with the eyes? If you see with all your senses, it has quite a different élan, quite a different depth and quite a different feeling.

Q: And yet such a looking is not fragmentary, it is not excluding.

K: Of course. When you watch something with all your senses—ears, eyes, taste, smell, touch—how can it be fragmentary? It is only when one particular sense dominates other senses that it is fragmentary. Can you as a teacher convey this to the students: to listen with all their capacity, with all their senses heightened? With most of us, one kind of sensation dominates the others, and therefore there is a sense of fragmentation. We do not seem to be able to see the totality of anything, or listen completely, with total attention.

We do not take life as a whole. Our life is fragmentary. If you are intellectual, you respect other intellects, and if others are not intellectual, you kind of shrug your shoulders or have contempt for them or despise them. So we never look at life as a whole movement. Or if one is romantic, sentimental and emotional, that again is a fragmentary activity. So, live a life totally, taking the whole movement of life as a unit that is in constant movement.

Can one do such a thing, when all our culture—education, society, religion—has divided the whole of life into the spirit, non-spirit, the good, the evil? Not only occasionally when you are by yourself in the hills or in the woods or listening to music, is it possible to treat life as a whole? That is, can one observe or see, listen and learn the whole movement of life non-fragmentarily?

Q: Does this mean that at each moment one somehow has a perspective which encompasses the whole of life?

K: Ah, no. Perspective is already fragmentary, isn't it? If you have a prospect, if you have a conception about what the whole of life is, that concept is put together by thought, and thought is in itself fragmentary, so therefore your perspective, conclusion, conceptual way of looking or trying to look at the whole of life will still be fragmentary. What does it mean to look at or to listen to something totally?

Q: Does it mean not to be paying attention to something else at the same time?

K: Sir, what is attention? To attend. It is a marvellous word, but what does it mean to attend? Is attention fragmentary, or is it concentration that is fragmentary? Concentration implies giving your energy to a particular thing, to centre upon something. In doing that, you exclude every other thought, movement. You put it away or resist or build a wall so that you can concentrate, centre upon that. Is attention like that? When you attend, it means you give all your energy; it is non-fragmentary if it is all one. When you attend to something completely, is there a fragmentation? When you concentrate, it is from a centre. When you attend, there is no centre.

I do not know if you have gone into the question of diligence and negligence. To be diligent, originally in Sanskrit, Latin, and so on, meant to be diligent in the service of God; to be diligent and not to be negligent; to give your attention, give your life, give everything you have. Negligent is not to pay attention at all. Concentration is negligence. To be diligent is to give complete attention.

If I had a student, I would want to convey to him that life is a whole movement, not a fragmentary movement, not an intellectual, emotional, romantic, idealistic, fragmentary movement. I would want to convey to him that life is a whole, harmonious activity. But he is already trained, educated, conditioned to function and live in fragments. So I have to deal with a mind that is already broken-up. How shall I do it? How shall I proceed with that?

This is exactly what is happening between us. How shall I proceed? How shall I tell you, not only verbally, not to convince you or do propaganda, but to awaken the mind to attend, be diligent? How shall I set about it?

Q: Point out the inattention?

K: All right, you point out the fragmentary. Then what? Then the mind will say, 'Now I must not be fragmentary, I must bring about an integration among the fragments, I must integrate myself'. It is a meaningless phrase.

So how would you convey this to your son, your daughter, your student? How would you show that life must be treated as a whole and therefore as sacred? The word whole means healthy, sane; not irrational, not neurotic, but completely sane. It also means holy, sacred. The word whole implies all that. Now, how will you convey this to your students, if you feel that life is one, is a total movement, not fragmentary? It is fragmentary when I assert myself, when I push my own personality, my own desires forward.

Q: Is it not fragmentary as soon as there is a self to assert?

K: Of course. I want to impress you with my knowledge, if I have that knowledge, and it would be fragmentary. How shall an educator convey it to the students to be attentive? When one is attentive all the senses are in operation. What will you do?

Q: Sir, could it be done through spontaneous action?

K: The word spontaneous means to act without restraint, without premeditation, without a goal, without a motive. To be spontaneous is one of the most difficult things, when our minds are so heavily conditioned.

Take a little time and look at this question. How will you convey to me verbally the feeling, the actuality that life, living, though broken up by human beings, is a total movement? How will you teach me? Teach me, meaning convey to me, tell me. Does it mean anything to you as an educator to tell me? Does the word whole mean anything to you, or is it just a word? The word implies physically healthy, sane, which means non-contradictory. Sanity: balance, harmony is implied in the word sanity, and holiness, sacredness. Not all that business in the churches and temples, but sane living itself is sacred. Does that word whole mean anything to you? Not just the word but the depth of it, the feel of it, the truth of it. Or is it merely an intellectual concept which you are going to think over and argue about? You can write volumes about it, and yet not be whole.

You listened to that word, and the content of that word. The deep significance of that word has been explained. Did you listen to it? Did you pay complete attention to it, or are you dissecting the word? 'What does he mean by health? What does he mean by sanity, by holy?' Is your mind, which is thought, more active than the sensory attention?

Q: I am not sure what you mean by sensory attention. My mind is more active when you are talking.

K: I am asking you, when you listened to all this, the word whole, did you listen to it completely, or did your mind move away, not in attention but arguing with the word?

Q: Yes.

K: Why does the mind do that? Sir, let's look at it. Is it part of our education, part of the inclination to look at something with all of its ramifications? Is it that our intellect is cultivated much more than perception?

Q: So perception is something different from the intellect?

K: What do you mean by the word intellect? It means to understand, to analyse, to have the capacity to dissect, to put things in their place, and so on. Is that what we are trying to do? That is what we have done with life. We have said there is the businessman, there is the politician, there is the artist, there is the poet, the painter, the cook, the chief; we have broken it all up. They have their function, but with the function goes status; the president is much more important than the gardener. Status has become more important than function. When you listen to the word whole, you are breaking it up, hoping thereby to understand the significance, the depth of that word. Aren't you doing that? When the word whole is used and the meaning of that word is given, you do not say, 'By

Jove, how true that is'. You do not feel it, you do not immediately capture the truth of it.

Q: Sir, we try to interpret the word, and by this very process of trying to interpret and capture the meaning, we try to make time stop.

K: When you are doing all this, the factor of time enters, as you pointed out. Time becomes a factor of understanding, of perceiving, of listening, or learning the art of listening, cultivating the art of listening. All that implies time. I will learn how to listen at the end of the month. That is what the student has been taught. You do not capture the truth of it instantly.

As an educator in a school of this kind, where the parents, the teachers are responsible for education, how am I to convey it to the student that time is not a factor in understanding, that time is not a factor in the art of listening?

Let's make it much more simple. I am your student. You are telling me something, and I look out of the window. What do you do? You want to tell me something very serious, and I look at that bird going by. What is the relationship between you and me then? How would you deal with that; as a teacher, what would you do?

Q: I would look also, sir.

K: What will you do with me, I said, not what will you do. I am your student, what will you do with me when you want to tell me something really whole—which is really quite extraordinary if you go into it? I look out of the window, how will you deal with me?

Q: Well, obviously you cannot force him to come back to what you are talking about.

K: That is understood. Move from there, sir.

Q: You point out that he should see. Perhaps ask him questions about what he saw.

K: You are dealing with me; do it now. I am your student. You want to tell me the meaning of the word whole, and I look out of the window and count the birds on that wire. What will you do? What is your action?

Q: I would try to help him see that he had a new attention, so to speak, that he had fragmented.

K: It is much simpler than that, sir. Why do you complicate everything?

To you the word whole means sacred, something holy. And you want to tell me that because it is very important in my life. If in my life there is nothing holy, then I am dead from the beginning to the end. So you want to convey this to me, you want to print it on my mind, and I am looking out of the window or talking to somebody.

If you are the educator how will you deal with me? Wouldn't you forget sacred, forget wholeness, and ask me to give complete attention to what I am seeing? Not create a division, not force me, not tell me I am not paying attention. Whereas if you say, 'Look at that bird you are watching. Give complete attention to it. Look at it with all your being, with all your senses. See all the feathers, how it is moving, the tender legs, the claws, the beak. Give your complete attention to it', it is finished! Right?

Are you doing that when we talk about it? When the speaker says the word whole, and that it means holy, are you giving your complete attention to it, or is your mind saying, 'What is whole? Is it a collection of fragments? Is it something he has invented and is putting meanings into?'

Sir, you are helping the student to attend. Whether he attends to the bird or to you is irrelevant. What is important is that he should attend.

Q: I understand.

K: So you have created in the student a feeling that whatever he does he must attend.

Q: I grasped what we needed to do. But when the bird flies away then the student's attention will be going elsewhere, so do you continually keep saying, 'See it'?

K: Go into it, sir. Is the bird making him attend, or he has the quality of attention? Is the bird forcing him to attend, or is he caught up in the looking? Do you see the difference? You give a child a toy, and the toy absorbs him because the toy is very interesting. The toy is so interesting that he is caught up in that. Take away the toy and he is lost. So are we grown-up people also caught up in interest in a toy, in an ideal, in a belief, and so on, or do we have the feeling of attention without the object?

Q: This process of attention in the child that you just described, isn't that a natural process?

K: We are not discussing natural, unnatural. You see, you are off to something. I am telling you something. You have seen children, sir. Give them a toy, and they are not mischievous; the child forgets, the toy takes him over. Take away the toy, he returns back to his mischief, crying, whatever he does. Are we also like that? Take away my business, I am lost; I become neurotic, or I do something idiotic. Things take over man. Take away knowledge, art, music, and he is lost, like the child. So, can you live a life without toys? If you want to go into this, it leads you to such depths.

Q: It seems to me that we are talking about how the child learns this particular quality of attention.

K: We are helping him to attend; not just to what you are saying. If he has the capacity to attend, he will listen to you. So we want to find out how to help the student to attend; not to the birds, to geography, to history, to mathematics, and so on, but to have the feeling of attention.

Q: So, to state this maybe a little differently, isn't the question in dealing with the child how to have the capacity to attend come about?

K: Sir, just look. What does the brain want? What is its necessity? Apart from food, nourishment, all that, what is its complete demand?

Q: Security?

K: Isn't it?

Q: Yes.

K: To be safe. To have complete security. This is within yourself, if you have observed. I am not a scientist or a neurologist or a brain expert; I just watch myself and watch people. The brain demands total security. There is no argument about it. Now, does society offer complete security?

Q: Obviously not.

K: Does education offer complete security?

Q: No.

K: Does religion offer complete security?

Q: No.

K: So, what are you offering him?

Q: Nothing.

K: No, no. Look, I am your student. My brain needs complete safety, security. It needs a sense of safety, security. Neither society, nor education, nor religion, nor politics offers that. Watch your own mind, sir. What does it do? If society, education, religion do not give him security, what does he do?

Q: Well, the mind faces the fact that there is no security.

K: Which is the most dangerous thing to admit to itself, because then it collapses, commits suicide, or becomes a vegetable, gives up everything. You know, you have seen people like that. What does it do?

Q: Sir, does the brain try to create securities of its own?

K: Doesn't it?

Q: Yes.

K: Either in some imaginative pictures, or it goes back to something in childhood and lives there or in some ideal, in some neurotic concepts and fancies.

Q: Daydreams.

K: Yes, daydreams, a dozen ways.

Q: So the question then becomes how the brain gets out of that.

K: Ah, no. Not out of it. How to prevent this happening; how to prevent this kind of false, imaginative security leading to illusion? Mental hospitals are filled with this. I have a student, I have a son, a daughter, and I want to prevent this now, not after it has happened. What shall I do? I want to prevent them from indulging in some form of fanciful illusion, or an illusion which is deeply satisfying, in which they think, 'At least, here I am safe'. I do not want them to go through that door, which leads to hell. I want to stop it. What shall I do?

Q: The state of complete attention automatically stops it.

K: No sir, forget attention. Think of it anew. What shall I do? You are faced with this, sirs. It is your problem. The parents are caught in some illusion. They believe: 'I am a Hindu. I am better than anybody else', and so on. What shall I do? The parents are like this, the educators are like this, and the poor student is caught in that. What am I to do with a student? How shall I close the door on all this?

(Pause)

What does the brain want—no, what must it have? Apart from air, food, and so on, what must it have?

Q: Security.

K: Complete security. Right?

Q: Right.

K: Why do you say there is no security in religion? Why do you say it is not secure in the priest, in the enormous structure of two thousand years of Christianity, the worship of Jesus, the whole business of it? Why isn't there security in the rituals, the dogma, the authority of two thousand years?

Q: Because it is an illusion that the mind itself has created.

K: Why do you say there is no security in organized religion, in this business? Why do you say it? Is it instant perception or from calculated intellectual investigation that you say that it is rubbish?

Why do you say that society does not give security, that culture—pictures, statues, books—does not give security? Is it intelligence or is it a calculated, intellectual rationalization, which is not intelligence?

Q: I see what you are saying.

K: Sir, in the long valley of the Nile, the ancient Egyptians said, 'We live in the cause of eternity'. To them it was everlasting, endless, for three, four, five thousand years. And they came to an end. There was no security there. So what makes educated human beings say there is no security in all this? What makes you say that? Go on, sir, what makes you say it?

Q: Simply that one has not found it.

K: No. What makes you say that in the structure of two thousand years of Christianity, two thousand years of worship, there is no security? What makes you say it?

Q: Sir, it is obvious: because it is based on a belief, it is based on imagination.

K: Have you dissected it, read the Christian Church history—all the trickery, all the torture, all the ambition, falsification—and therefore you say, 'It is all rubbish'?

Q: Intelligence can tell one without having to investigate it.

K: Do you say that in religions as they are there is no security?

Q: Yes.

K: And do you say the same thing with regard to culture, business; that in the whole social, economic, religio-social structure as it is now, there is no security? Then what has happened to your brain? When it says there is nothing in that, what happens to your brain?

Q: You do not pursue it any more.

K: I know you do not, but what happens to it? What has happened to it?

Q: Your brain is clear. You can really see. You have thrown it all out.

K: No. It has a shock. When you have put your whole investment in all that, and suddenly it collapses, what happens to you?

Q: It is a shock.

K: It is a shock. Then what do you do? You are not facing the thing in yourself.

Q: You start searching for security in another area maybe.

K: The brain needs to have complete security. It has found no security in anything. What has created religion, the structure?

Q: Thought.

K: So, are you saying there is no security in thought?

Q: Yes.

K: No, no, please, do not agree. There is no security in knowledge, which has been put together by thought, by investigation, accumulation of scientific knowledge, archaeological knowledge. There is no security in anything that thought has created. So what do you do? When you realize there is no security in anything—in the relationship between man and woman, between two people, in anything that thought has put together, however sublime, however beautiful, however lovely, good—what happens?

Q: Sir, you have to rely on yourself then.

K: Ah no! You are the result of thought. No? What happens? Watch your own mind, sir, please.

Q: You are insecure.

K: Are you?

Q: No, you are secure. When you realize that none of these things give you security, a security occurs.

K: Does it, or are you just saying a non-actuality? Be very strict and scrupulous in this. What happens to a mind which has realized that in all the things it has invested, hoping for security, there is no security? When it comes to the point that there is no security of any kind in thought itself and all the structures, all the beauty, all the things that thought has created, what happens to the brain?

Q: There is an experience of liberation, but it seems that thought continues.

K: Liberation from what?

Q: Liberation from the conception that the patterns of thought are one's own.

K: Is it an actuality, or just a theory that you are spinning around? Have you no more vested interest in anything that thought has created? Just go slowly. This is a tremendous thing that we are saying.

I realize that my brain, this brain, this human brain which is the result of growth in time of a million years and more, must have complete security. Otherwise it cannot function properly; otherwise, with most people, it deteriorates with old age; or it becomes neurotic; or it gets hurt, spoiled, destroyed. That is a fact. And thought has invested its security in all those things, and it suddenly realizes that in none of those things, ever, is there security. Not periodically, ever! In my relationship with my wife, with my children, in nothing is there security. What happens to the brain? What takes place inside your brain? You do not face it. It is a great shock, a tremendous shock to realize that it has invested all its life in something that is absolutely empty, worthless; that it has invested its security in ashes.

Q: Then your mind is free.

K: No, no, it is not free.

Q: You stop thinking. It is quiet.

K: Is it a shock to you, or are you just playing with words? We are dealing with something enormous and you are playing with things.

What happens? What takes place naturally is that, when you have invested a hundred thousand dollars in a stock, and it crashes, you are shocked. Either you jump from the twentieth floor or you say, 'My God!' Right? You do not play with it. It is a tremendous shock. Then what is important is what happens after the shock. During the state of shock there is a certain paralysis. If you fall down, there is a shock, there is a certain paralysis. If there is a motor accident, there is shock, paralysis. The mind for the moment is paralyzed. What happens in the next moment is all-important: how the mind comes out of that shock. Will it be shocked permanently, or is there a resilience, a new birth, a new saying: 'There is no security, therefore...'? But the mind must have security.

Q: Sir, isn't there a difference between needing security and seeking security? The mind needs it.

K: Yes. The mind needs security, and it seeks security in all these things. Now it has discovered that in none of those things is there any security. But it needs it. I have searched in this and this and this, and I thought I had found security in God. But the communists or the analysts say, 'Oh that is just an invention, a fantasy'. And I go back again. So, as I said, knowing it must have complete security, how it comes out of that shock is all-important.

I have invested security in my money, in all these things. But when I see there is no security there, I am going to invest in myself. I am going to have confidence in myself, in my knowledge, in the things I have gathered. Then the reaction is: 'If it is not there, it is in here, inside. God is inside. God is not out there, it is inside'. The ancient Hindus have done this very well. 'It is inside, and I am going to find that inside'; control thought. The movement out there is now the same movement inside.

Look, I have discovered something. As long as there is a movement out there or in here, there is no security. I have sought security in churches, temples, beliefs, wealth, knowledge, books, business. It is in none of that. I sought security in my wife; she moves somewhere else, so I am lost. I went outward looking for security; after the shock of seeing it is not there, the reaction is to go inward. This is a natural reaction. I do not say, 'It stops. It is free'. The natural reaction is: I have not found it out there, so I hope to find it inside. So I begin the same old game again, seeking security in my belief, in my experience. It is the same movement, only turned inward. So I realize that any movement, whether out there or in here, is essentially insecure.

Q: That means any movement towards security.

K: Any movement. Out there, in here; any movement. Which is, any movement in the search for security. I moved into the world of propaganda, churches, business, investment in stocks, or communism. I moved there hoping to find some kind of security. And I am now 80, 50, 30, and I have not found any security. The natural reaction is to go inward: 'I must have confidence in myself, in my experience. I relied on the experience of others before, now I am relying on my experience'. Which is the same as the other. Is there a doubt about that?

Q: What about a movement in the direction of understanding oneself, particularly by means of understanding what you talk about?

K: Yes. That is, I have turned inward: 'If I can understand myself completely, I will have security'.

Q: Precisely.

K: Now, instead of investing security out there I am investing it in here.

Q: I am investing it in self-understanding.

K: Yes. Call it by any name you like. I have abandoned investment in the Church, now I invest in the State, in the totalitarian state. If that does not come off, I invest in investigating into myself. I am talking of investment, not into what. The objects of investment are the same, whether they are out there or in here.

Q: Because it is thought that created both. You thought the outside, and now you have turned your thought inside.

K: It is exactly the same thing. Thought said I will find security out there. Since it has not found it, in reaction thought says I will find it in here. And much later on, it says I have not found it there either. I realize with a great shock that the reaction is the same as action. I have discovered something very good: reaction is the same as action. So, where is security?

Q: It is in your discovery that action is the same as reaction.

K: I have discovered it, not you. Do not invest in my discovery.

So, if action and reaction are the same, then what? Do not forget that the brain must have complete security. There is no security out there; there is no security inside. It says there is no security in any kind of movement. So, what is that which is without movement? Because all time is movement. All time is movement. All thought is movement in time and measure. And what is there without movement? Which means, what is there without time?

I am putting the questions, you are not. You are gathering information from me, in which you are going to find security. And I am saying: what is there without time, without movement? Is there anything? Or is there nothing?

How am I going to convey all this to my poor students? I want to convey all this to them, because this is life—complete life, not just bread and butter or sex or church or business. This is complete life. I want them to understand the beauty and the depth of this. How shall I do it, what shall I do? I want to help them to have no investment in all that, nor in all this. And they do not know even the beginnings of it. They do not know even the distant smell of it. So what shall I do?

I have to begin with attention: 'Attend! If you are interested in looking out of that window, for God's sake look out of that window. But look with all your eyes so that you have no contradiction in yourself'. In himself and therefore with his teacher. You help me. You say, 'Look! Look! Do not pay attention to what I am saying for the moment, but look. And see how long you can look. Is it a short look and then you jump to something else? If it is a short look, next time find out how long you can look. With attention that is not forced'. And when he has looked out of the window, and you have helped him to look out of the window, then when you say, 'Now listen to me', he will. Do you have it? But if you say, 'Oh, do not look out of the window, pay attention', then you are gone up the chimney.

Q: So, implied in this is that the student will reach some point at which he will know that he is not attentive.

K: Sir, I do not want him to know or not know. I want him to find out. I want him to find out that when he is inattentive, that is the dangerous moment. Driving when he is inattentive may cause an accident. It is the state of inattention which modern education has given us, that is destroying everything—the world, everything. So you help the student to have this extraordinary feeling of attention: at the table, to how he eats, when he greets somebody; the whole of it.

After all, the whole of life is love and death, isn't it? The whole of life includes all of this: suffering, pleasure, fear, love and death. I want him to understand the whole thing. And meditation. How do you explain death to him? What do you say to a student who says, 'What is death? I see that bird die, the cat ate it. I see the way whales are being killed. What is death?' How do you deal with that?

And how do you deal with meditation? They must have heard this word, especially now in this country. In India, when I go to the schools there, at the end of a talk or discussion I say, 'Sit still'. Immediately, that second, they cross their legs, sit absolutely still. Little boys! It is part of their tradition. It comes naturally to sit still. Now, how do you explain to the students what meditation is?

Do you see, sirs? This is the whole of life, including love, hate; what does love mean, is it sex, is it pleasure? People have talked about love of Jesus—and they have killed each other.

Q: Can one cultivate knowing, or cultivate being aware when one is inattentive, without turning that into the idea or concept that I am going to pay attention?

K: No. That is not attention, is it? Just see it. I am going to pay attention. That is in the future. Therefore you are not attentive now. Which means you are inattentive now.

Find something out. When you use the words going to be, that involves time. That is the process of cultivating something. Here, the cultivation is to be attentive. Is attentiveness a factor of time? We must be quite sure. When you are completely attentive, there is no time.

Q: Can you cultivate an awareness of when you are not attentive, when you are in that factor of time?

K: No, I would not use the word cultivate. Cultivate implies time. I cultivate the garden; I plant something, it takes time to grow.

Q: Can we bring about an awareness?

K: Attention has no time. It is not a factor of time. If there is time, then it is not attention. Either I listen to you now or I do not listen to you. It is not that I am going to listen to you when it is convenient for me, when I am not looking out of the window. Attention implies the total elimination of time. There is no time involved at all in attention. Wherever there is inattention there is time; there is, 'I will do something about it'. To be aware that I am inattentive is to be attentive. I do not have to cultivate it.

Attention is a state where inattention does not exist. Where there is inattention, I am going to do something: 'I will learn', But while I am learning a language, I do not say, 'I am going to learn'. I am learning. Attention is the state where time does not exist. Inattention is our trouble.

I do not realize that I am inattentive. I cannot force myself to realize it; that only cultivates further inattention because I am going to learn to be attentive.

I want to convey this to the students. I would say, 'When you look at a bird, or look at a tree, look at it. Pay complete attention at the moment'; not 'I am going to pay attention'. When your mind goes from the tree to the picture on the wall, pay attention to that. And from the picture, it goes to something else. Be aware of this constant movement'. That is attention.

There is no friction, there is no conflict in this. We are bred on conflict: 'You must pay attention, you must concentrate'. You eliminate all that when you say, 'If you are giving attention, give it'.

SOURCES

J. Krishnamurti in dialogue with parents, teachers and trustees in Ojai, California.

1. Understanding what it means to learn.	*6 December 1975*
2. Bringing about a totally different kind of mind.	*13 December 1975*
3. Can a human being live without conflict?	*20 December 1975*
4. Transformation in the depth of human beings.	*3 January 1976*
5. Is my relationship to my student a conceptual one?	*10 January 1976*
6. Is it possible to have intelligence without experience?	*17 January 1976*
7. The pure act of learning.	*24 January 1976*
8. Caring.	*31 January 1976*
9. To be totally responsible.	*7 February 1976*
10. How will you educate the student not to be hurt?	*14 February 1976*
11. Can I help the student to listen?	*21 February 1976*
12. To be diligent is to give complete attention.	*28 February 1976*